ALL THAT GLITTER
IS NOT
GOLD

Marilyn M. Lowery
with Kenneth P. Cash

ALL THAT GLITTER IS NOT GOLD

Copyright © 2014 by Marilyn M. Lowery and Kenneth P. Cash

Layout and Design: Ileta Randall

Cover Design: James D. Jones

ISBN: 978-1-938950-32-2

Greater Is He Publishing
9824 E. Washington St., Chagrin Falls, Ohio 44023
P. O. Box 46115, Bedford, Ohio 44146
http://www.greaterishepublishing.com
216-288-9315

Dedication

This Book Is Dedicated To My Legacy

Felicia
My Eldest Daughter

Melissia
My Middle Daughter

Khaleedah
My Youngest Daughter

Table of Contents

Preface

According to Ms. Marilyn M. Lowery, all of the events and circumstances discussed in this book are true accounts that really happened, including the details, happening in the ways that are related.

From the information that Ms. Marilyn Lowery has imparted to me about herself and her life, I am in awe of her resiliency after suffering several severely dramatic experiences in her life, some of which were beyond her control and some, results of her decisions. Her life has been full of riveting drama, but ultimately, she has emerged triumphantly. In addition to the fascinating reading of these gripping accounts and the enlightened knowledge that can be gained from reading about these happenings, I think that her responses and determined behavior to these spellbinding occurrences can serve as an inspiration to other people who may experience any of these specific events and/or circumstances.

All of my written input for this book has been my pleasure. All of my writing that is contained in this book is a result of information as provided to me by Ms. Marilyn M. Lowery. I may or may not agree with any or all of the perceptions, opinions, and statements about any of the individuals, groups of people, and/or institutions expressed in this book. Also, the statements in this book may or may not reflect the perceptions and opinions of Seekers Publishing, Inc. In relating the true events and circumstances expressed in this book as related to me by Ms. Marilyn M. Lowery, the names of many people are stated in the book. In some instances, the real names of these people are expressed in this book, and the names of certain other individuals have been changed. With regards to all names that are articulated in this book, actual or changed names, anyone else whose name may be the same as any of the names stated in this book, living or dead, is entirely coincidental. It is not my and Seekers Publishing, Inc.'s deliberate intention to in any way injure any person, group of people, or institution.

Kenneth P. Cash

Kenneth P. Cash

Introduction

I am writing this book to inform people that anyone can go to prison, so never say it will never happen to you because we know where we have been, but we do not know where we are going.

My inspiration for writing this book is from having been a wife, model, and being a mother who became a prison inmate for twenty-two years.

I am writing this book for several additional reasons. Firstly, I desire to share information with everyone who really wants to know what happened to me. I want the family of my co-defendant's victim who was killed to know what really happened. We all know that the people present at the robbery and murder lied about me because I have NEVER owned a gun in my life, nor did I have one that night at the crime scene. The only gun that I have ever dealt with was my co-defendant's gun. I really did not have anything to do with the actual murder of that man. I was not even in the room when he was murdered, but I am very sorry that he was killed, and I express my condolences to his family and to anyone who may have been negatively affected by his passing away.

I am also writing this book for my now deceased parents and for my three daughters just in case they have any small doubt in their minds about their mother. I am sure that my brothers and sisters also wonder what happened. I am just trying to put everyone's mind at ease about what happened to me, Marilyn Lowery.

Furthermore, I think that the information presented in this book will enlighten judges, prosecutors, the court system, and will further expose domestic abuse regarding women and men of all ages in our society. Moreover, this book will inform taxpayers that part of their money is used to take care of prisoners until inmates are released from prison.

I am hoping that perhaps someone will provide me with the necessary assistance to create a movie about a woman, me, who took twenty-two years to tell her life story of mental abuse, unwise drug abuse, the court system, and the parole board that I think tried to keep me incarcerated to continue to receive several thousands of dollars by violating my constitutional rights, and this practice also affected many other prison inmates.

Overall, I hope that this book will be an inspiration to women and men.

Marilyn M. Lowery

Chapter One

My Husband's Murder
and
My Mental Response

All of my troubles started on the USA's Bicentennial night – July 4, 1976. I was twenty years old, and my husband was twenty-one. My darling husband, Edward D. Lowery, Jr., had purchased tickets for us to attend his friend's party. We enjoyed the festivities and later went to a local disco, the King's Inn, on Payne Avenue in Cleveland, Ohio. The evening had evolved into night, a *dark* night as I would soon discover! We ventured out into the darkness to my car.

My husband had been acting strangely all week, including that evening, making comments that led me to wonder where is he going and telling me how much he loved me. I think now that maybe somehow he felt his imminent death.

Long before that night, I had asked God to reveal the future to me. He did! Two weeks prior to my husband's untimely demise, I dreamed of his death. In my dream, he had been shot and killed! At that time, I didn't understand as my husband was not a gangster, carried no gun or anything like that. His death was the first vision God had given to me. Also, not long before this tragic night, my husband had taken my two daughters, Felicia and Missy, and me to visit his father who lived in Youngstown, Ohio. My older daughter, Felicia, who at that time was only six years old, brought back with her a book titled *Where Do the Dead Go?* by Jehovah's Witnesses. That book stayed on my mind.

On that somber July 4th night after our King's Inn visit, we were journeying home in my car. At that time, it was around 2:00 a.m. on July 5, 1976. My adored husband was driving while I sat in the front, passenger seat beside him. My sister was sitting in the car's back seat behind my husband. As my husband was driving down Payne Avenue around East 45th Street in Cleveland, he had his window open about only one inch. As the car was moving, I heard what sounded like firecrackers which are what I first thought they were. Turning my head in my husband's direction, I saw that his head had fallen backwards onto the top of the seat. He had been struck in the back of his head by the first bullet, spraying his brains and blood all over my sister sitting behind him! The second bullet had ricocheted off of the car's roof. I immediately exclaimed in horror to my brains-spattered, blood-drenched sister, "Ed's been shot!"

At the moment of impact, my husband's foot was on the accelerator, and the car's speed greatly increased. As the car sped really fast, I yelled to my sister, "Girl, we gotta try da stop this car!" My sister lunged her arms over the seat, grabbing the steering wheel in an attempt to prevent the car from reeling out of control as I tugged my husband's foot to disengage it from the accelerator. At that time, the horn on my car was not working. My Ford Mustang barreled through the intersection of East 55th Street and Payne Avenue and the red traffic light and bounded over the curb and into a vacant field where it came to rest. As I cradled my dying husband in my arms, my sister jumped out of the car to flag down some people who summoned a policeman. It all seemed like a horrifying movie to me, but it was real! My precious husband, unconscious and whose eyes by that time had become largely swollen, was rushed to Charity Hospital, a nearby medical facility, where a doctor told me, "Mrs. Lowery, your husband is not going to live." Then the doctor asked me if I wanted to have my husband's organs donated. Being young and in shock then, I didn't know the importance of organ donation. I thought, "If you take out his organs, then I know he will die for sure," so I declined.

In retrospect, I think that the killer must have used a

rifle with a telescopic sight to hit who he aimed at while the car was in motion and not breaking the glass in my husband's slightly opened car window.

A man working at the New Lounge Bar was convicted of murdering my husband. The police claimed that the crime was racially motivated. Crime investigators must have had their reasons for believing that this man had committed the crime. I guess one of the reasons that would fit the post-behavior of some people who have committed a crime is that he did leave the Cleveland, Ohio, area soon after the shooting took place, but I don't know for sure why he left. For his alleged crime, he was sentenced to serve a fifteen-years-to-life prison sentence. Years later when he and I were in different prisons for unrelated crimes, I found out where and how to contact him by letter. He responded by letter telling me that he was innocent of killing my husband, and I tend to believe him, I guess just because of the way he presented his statement. I wondered if the incident had anything to do with the law suit my husband had against the company for which he worked and was soon to get a large settlement from that company. However, to this day I do not know for sure why or who murdered my husband.

Emotionally, I was devastated by my husband's forced exit from my life, and what added to his absence from me was the suddenness in which he was taken out of my earthly life. My husband's passing away so overwhelmingly shattered me emotionally that I suffered my first nervous breakdown. For months afterwards, I didn't want to live, but I pulled myself together for the sake of my precious children. Still, even years later, I was deeply affected by the end of my relationship with him and would sometimes suffer time periods of depression. I was lonely and missed my adored husband. When a person sees anyone killed, that viewer thinks about it most frequently, but when a woman sees her husband killed right in her presence, that event is a nightmare that she will never never forget.

My Loving Husband and Me

My Childhood Home

Chapter Two

My Childhood Through Young Adulthood Years

I came from a family that consisted of a mother, father and nine siblings – five boys and five girls, including me. I am the fifth oldest having two older brothers and two older sisters. I also have two brothers and two sisters who are younger than me. My parents were born in southeastern Virginia in a town called Newport News which is the same town where I was born in 1955. My family, including me, moved to Cleveland, Ohio, when I was seven or eight years old. I can well remember when my parents obtained their house on East 84th Street and Superior Avenue in Cleveland, Ohio. Neither of my parents finished school. I think that both of them completed school up to only the sixth grade, but they always pushed all of us, my brothers and sisters and me, to go to school. In some ways I liked school, but in other ways I didn't.

As a child, I remember one time there was a little fire in our basement. I told one of my sisters to go upstairs and tell our mother; however, my sister wouldn't, so later I told our mother that my sister had caused the fire. I also remember that as a child, I would sometimes lie on grass on a warm day with a nice breeze and think about things, never really thinking about what I wanted to be. One thing for sure – I never thought that I would be a prison inmate someday.

My father worried about his children. When we were young and sometimes playing outdoors in the evenings and it was bedtime, my father would come out of the house and call all of his children into the house. We'd tell our friends, "I've got to go; see you tomorrow." My father was a laborer and occasionally drank to excess and would verbally "fuss," talk "off the wall" stuff. My mother never worked a job and had no vices – did not smoke, etc. She seemed to have a remarkable talent for raising children – ten of her own, my three daughters, and other children.

I was like many school-aged children when growing up; I occasionally "cut" school and experimented with the popular recreational drugs at the time such as cocaine, "mes," "meth," "hash," "Black Beauties," LSD aka "acid," and smoked marijuana to name some. I was curious as to how these drugs would make me feel. They heighten your senses and make you do crazy, potentially dangerous things. I remember that while under the influence of one of these substances, I felt like jumping out of a window. The distance was not far down, but when you are on drugs, it seemed like fifty stories up. I remember another time I was sitting in a chair in a vacant field filled with trash, old things.

Recreational drugs can destroy a person's life.

After a high comes a low; these harmful drugs cause a person to feel tired, irritable, depressed, and produces paranoia, sleep problems, anxiety along with problems with a person's heart and blood pressure. In short, after having experienced many of these illegal drugs, they can really cause a person problems, and as far as I am concerned, the harmful results are not worth the temporary "high" that these drugs produce. In the long run, these drugs just cause a person more stress than he or she would normally have, and enough can go wrong with a person's body naturally without volunteering to increase and in some cases cause physical and mental problems. Continued use of these drugs can destroy a person's life. When I was taking these drugs, I didn't want my mother to know about this behavior, so when I would go home, I went to bed to sleep. Similarly, I

6

did not tell my sisters about my reckless behavior because I didn't want to be bothered. I was in a world of my own. I also drank whatever I felt like drinking. I ended up quitting school after completing the ninth grade. I knew at the time that I was just hanging around with the wrong crowd, but I thought that I was just going to be a child one time so I'd enjoy that period of time in my life that way. I wanted to be an adult at the time so I could do whatever I wanted whenever I felt like it. I began "messing around" with boys. However, I was never sexually involved with a boyfriend I had when I was fifteen years old, and he was older than my parents; he was seventy-eight years old and married. He used to lavish me with expensive gifts. Nevertheless, I continued living in my parents' house until I was seventeen years old. I had my first child, a girl, when I was fifteen years of age. My first child was my parents' first grandchild. I got married when I was seventeen years old and also had my second child, with the same man as my first child, when I was that same age, seventeen years. At that time, this man was my loving husband. I did not think about school after that; my only concern was to be a good mother to my two wonderful children. Furthermore, I quit using these potentially harmful drugs as I had matured and now had the responsibilities of raising two cherished children. I was married to my husband from age seventeen years to twenty years of age until my dear husband was suddenly killed. After my husband had passed away, I became a mental mess but never sought professional help. The last lovely child I had was when I was serving time in prison, in 1982. This daughter, my youngest child's father was my co-defendant. Now I have three exceedingly wonderful daughters for whom I have endless love.

During my twenties, between the births of my second and third daughters, I was a fashion model. When I was younger, I liked seeing nice clothes. Then later when I was a young adult, I attended a modeling school, and for awhile I was a make-up artist instructor. I thought that maybe I would eventually be discovered by someone and become famous. Once someone from a modeling agency wanted to use me for modeling, but I would have had to cut my hair which I did not want to do then, so I declined the modeling offer. Even though I had an agent, I then freelanced, doing some fashion shows. When I participated in modeling shows, the sponsors had specific clothes that they wanted me to wear. However, on my own, I would go to places like the Good Will and to "regular" stores, finding clothing items and putting them together. My second daughter, then very young, remembers that when I would practice modeling, she and her sister would be my audience sometimes. I would repeatedly walk into a room, each time wearing a different outfit, and they would clap. This same daughter remembers, "When she (my mother) would walk out of the house, she would look like a movie star." During my modeling years, I invested much money into that endeavor – going to modeling school and creating and building a modeling portfolio. After modeling for two or three years, I did not think that I was going anywhere in that field, so I abandoned it.

However, I love my clothing very much and would like to open a clothing and make-up store, all in one, because every woman wants to look beautiful regardless of her age, young or old. All of my life I wanted so many things. For example, I love to sew outfits together, but I have never had the money or the connections to realize these desires that I have envisioned.

9

Chapter Three

As A Widow, Supermodel, Mother, and Wife, My
Involvement With Another Man

Although five years had passed since my loving
husband had suddenly and shockingly exited this world, I
still suffered time periods of depression from the absence of
my wonderful relationship with him. In the summer of 1981,
I was lured into what would lead into the worst part of my
life so far. During one of my depressive time periods, I met a
man who I considered attractive looking, a flashy dresser, as
having a smooth, charming manner, and had at least a little
financial means. I never loved him, but he appeared to be a
gentleman and exerted himself to be gracious with my two
children and me. He told me that he would care for and
protect me. At the time I was gullible and mostly illiterate, so I
believed him. I guess, during that time, I was an easy target
for his silver tongue and general appeal. I remember him
telling me once that he had a house in Canton, Ohio, but
that his wife and daughter had been killed in that house.

After months of keeping company with him, I saw the
other side to him – his mean side! One of his behaviors was
frequently slapping me around. For example, one time
when he thought that I was not making his dinner fast
enough, he hit me so hard that I feared that he had broken
my jaw. Although he never hit me in front of my daughters,
then aged ten and twelve years, they can remember many
times when they would hear brawling-type sounds and
screaming coming from behind the closed bedroom door. I
tried very hard to hide this man's abusive behavior towards
me from my two daughters because I was afraid that if my
children knew what was happening, they might tell
someone such as a teacher.

11

Right from the beginning of my association with this man, my perceptive mother saw through him and let her dislike of him known. Therefore, he first isolated me from my parents and then my children, and eventually my women friends, CLAIMING that my female friends were lesbians so he didn't want them around.

Moreover, he almost continuously threatened me with his .357 magnum gun. Also, sometimes he would just lay the gun out somewhere as if he were waiting for someone to break in. My two older daughters can remember him with a gun numerous times.

Fortunately my children were unaware of it, but he introduced me to hard drugs. His preference was cocaine and opium. I hated the smell of it. He eventually impelled me into prostitution, selling my body. One day he told me that he wants me to sell my body and when I agreed, he wanted me to go on a street corner. I just stood there and saw several other women stopping cars almost continuously. He became furious with me because I was not stopping cars and therefore began slapping me around right on the street that night. I knew that I had to do something somehow. I had become his prisoner. One example is that I could not even wear what I wanted to. *He* chose the clothes that I was supposed to wear. In March of 1982, I was arrested for prostitution which was my first apprehension by the law.

Then there was the recurrent name calling like "you no good bitch; no one would want you but me." He told me that if I left him, he would kill me or kill my children. By this time I was terrified of him.

On one occasion when I was not around, this terrifying monster began touching my oldest daughter and kissing her on her lips. Fortunately this daughter escaped but told no one but me about this occurrence. This incident happened only once, but I rhetorically ask, "How many times does it take to start molesting an adult and especially a child?"

I thought that the quickest way I could escape from this man was to move back in with my parents because I knew that my father would not let this man and I live together, unmarried, in my parents' house. Also, I thought that maybe my parents would see that something was wrong. I tried to hide from my family this man's abuse of my children and me because I was embarrassed and didn't know how to handle this situation with this man. However, I asked my mother if my two daughters and I could move in with them, my parents. My parents, not knowing the reason which was abuse, thought that I wanted to move back with them so that my mother could just babysit my two young daughters while I "ran the streets," so I abandoned the idea of trying to move back with my parents. I wasn't woman enough then to tell my mother that this man was abusing me. I had so many unanswered questions that I really didn't know who to talk with about the situation.

I felt like I was his prisoner in my own house and that I couldn't get away from him. He was exceedingly dominant and knew how to play to my vulnerabilities. Contemplating this capsulated information presented here may appear to be a clear case of abuse, but this behavior happened gradually over a period of time, and domestic violence was not widely or publicly discussed much at that time. At that time I didn't really know that I was being abused. I had never been in that kind of relationship before, and I knew that I wanted to escape from being in that horrible situation I was in with this man, but I did not know just how to escape from that relationship. A person does not know what some women go through unless the woman has been in the same kind of relationship. Maybe this abusive situation is much more obvious to outsiders, but when a person is actually immersed in a situation and the person's emotions are involved, the person's plight and obvious course of action to escape may not be so evident. Also then, there were not many places where women could go to for help. As miserable as prison was, perhaps going to prison saved my life since that caused me to be away from this beast.

I am sure that there are some other women in our society who have been and may presently be in a similarly abusive situation. I was lucky in being able to eventually exit from this horrific predicament, but there might be some other women who are not as fortunate in this way. My advice to those women is to seek help before it is too late!!!!

For anyone in an abusive relationship seek help before it is too late.

Chapter Four

The Crime

It was on the chilly evening of April 3, 1982, when Thomas had me drive him to the apartment complex where his mother lived. Previously at home, he had brought out, wiped clean and polished his .357 Magnum gun. I thought that maybe he was preparing to sell it. Before we left the house, he told me to get some paper bags. Sometimes he would take some food out of his mother's freezer, so I thought that that is what he had in mind to do. At the time I had no idea that he was planning to use the bags to hold other people's money. His mother lived in the upstairs portion of this building, and the after-hours joint was on the first floor. That night when my co-defendant and I went to this after-hours joint, he was wearing gloves which struck me as being rather peculiar, but I thought that maybe he wore gloves sometimes because after having been in prison, perhaps he was overly conscious about leaving his fingerprints about, so I guess I did not think anymore about him wearing gloves that evening. Instead of me driving into the parking lot of the building, he had me park the car on a side street a few blocks from the apartment. I thought that was rather strange but complied with his wish since there was a small driveway nearby.

Thomas and I walked to the building and entered where we saw the owner and one other person enjoying drinks. Thomas and I each had a drink. Then to my shocking surprise, Thomas pulled out his gun, announced that he was going to rob those present, ordered both of these people to take out their wallets, then made them go into another room and lie down onto the floor, face down. I was astonished! I was stunned! Thomas then ordered me to collect the two

15

people's money and the remaining liquor and to put these items into a bag. Scared out of my wits, I obeyed his command! It was like a dream. I could scarcely believe what was happening! Extremely frightened, I turned and headed for the door to exit the place. Just as I was about to leave, the door to this after-hours place opened and two more men walked in, later discovered to be LeMorris Terry and Curry "Junior" Thomas. Thomas ordered them into the front room and onto the floor also. At this point, I was able to gather enough thought together to know that I wanted no part of this event. I refused to participate any further, and I told Thomas that I was leaving. He wanted me to stay. Chills running down my spine, I said to him that I was leaving and that if he wanted to shoot me, that is what he'd have to do because I was leaving. Then someone else knocked on the door, and one more man walked into this place. When this man entered the spot, I left. I have to admit, I did walk out of the building with other people's money and liquor. There were four patrons there that night plus the owner. I did not know any of them except Thomas.

I hurried to the car, hardly believing what had just transpired, and got into the car. Sitting there nervously, I heard a shot! Then shortly after that, Thomas came running across a field and got into the car. He was puffing, ranting and glassy-eyed. I asked him, "What in the hell happened?" He replied that one of the victims began struggling with him, and his gun accidentally went off. We left in my father's car with me behind the wheel. Driving back home I could barely believe the whole incident! How could this be happening? I broke out into a cold sweat, so I started throwing the wallets out of the car, and I thought, "This is the man who I had been sleeping with every night." After we arrived home, he clamored that he wanted to get another gun and return to that after-hours spot and kill the remaining people there. I talked him out of it. At that time, I was living two houses from my parents. Using my father's car that night, I drove his car to my parents' house to return their car and gave the car keys back to my father who at that time was unaware of what had just taken place. When Thomas, who turned out to be my co-defendant, and I returned to the house where we were then residing, my co-defendant cut up the gloves he had been wearing and flushed them down the toilet and began drinking liquor straight down.

This devastating event occurred on a Saturday. Monday, I learned from reading about the incident in a newspaper that after I had left the after-hours spot, one of the victims said that while my co-defendant had his victims lying face down on the floor, my co-defendant became infuriated when one of the other victims had no money that my co-defendant could steal from him, so my co-defendant immediately shot this victim with no money in the back of his head, the bullet exiting one of his eyes, killing him instantly. The next victim telling what had happened said that after that other victim had been shot, he then jumped up saying that he did not want to die like that, grabbed the gun that my co-defendant was clasping, and the two men began struggling. The grapple went from the living room, down the hallway, into the kitchen. The victim was finally able to wrench the gun away from my co-defendant, my co-defendant dropping the gun in the kitchen. Then my co-defendant bolted from the kitchen and out of the building, vanishing into the darkness. However, the man who was running that after-hours joint then, knew my co-defendant and identified my co-defendant as the perpetrator of this crime to the policemen who had responded to this horrible disaster.

Later this victim said that I had pretended to have a gun during the robbery part of the incident by keeping a pointed finger in my pocket. The same victim did say though that I was already out of the building when my co-defendant shot dead the now deceased victim and that I was already gone when the two men battled each other. Unfortunately,

17

the police and the prosecutor's office believe that I did have a gun during the incident and was present when my co-defendant shot the victim. I wish to reaffirm what I have maintained all along which is that I never had a gun during that incident and was not present when my co-defendant shot and killed one of his victims. I have never owned a gun nor did I have a gun. My co-defendant wanted and tried to teach me how to use that gun, but I refused because that gun was not registered and could have been somehow used destructively somewhere else prior to my knowledge of that gun. I wanted no part of that gun.

I was captured first. One week prior to the incident, I was walking on a street wearing a mink coat. I had been a fashion model; I have an affinity for attractive-looking clothes and make-up. One of my dear daughters recalls that when she was a little girl, whenever I left the house, I looked like a movie star. I was just conscious about the way I looked. I was picked up by the police who said that I was soliciting. I was not motioning to or talking with any man nor was any man motioning to me. However, as a result of this apprehension, I was detained for one night in a jail. Thus, the police had my name and a photograph of me. Consequently, one week later when my co-defendant committed his crime, his mother was living above the after-hours establishment, so when he implemented his crime, his victims, knowing who he was, immediately identified him and told police where his mother was living. Then when the police asked his mother where he was, she replied that he was at some girl's house named Marilyn. My co-defendant's sister who was present at the time tried to thwart the police by telling them that my name was Marilyn Bell. Nevertheless, the police had remembered that they had arrested a woman named Marilyn a week prior, so they came looking for me for questioning. Now after the crime had occurred, I went to my mother's house, told her of the crime, at which time I had not yet known where the person in question had been shot and that he had passed away, having been murdered, and stayed at my mother's house. I did not know that one of my co-defendant's victims had passed away until I read about it in the newspaper the following Monday.

I ascertained that I would eventually be arrested, so I tried to prepare my two little daughters for that time. I told them that one day probably soon, I would be gone for awhile. The three of us were staying at my parents' house.

Then five days or so after the crimes of robbery and murder had occurred, a car slowly pulled into my driveway. Two detectives exited the car and approached my house. One of my brothers was on the front porch of my house. One of the investigators asked my brother where I was, so he showed them my parents' house two doors away. When the police found me there, they had a photograph of the crime committer with them. My mother was exceedingly scared and therefore wanted me to tell the police that I did not know the man in the photograph. Although I was exceedingly terrified, when the police asked me if I knew the man in the photograph, I replied, "Yes." Next, the police asked me that if I didn't mind, they would like me to come to the police station for further questioning. As a result, I never came back. I was incarcerated in one place or another from then on until I had served my prison sentence.

At the time that I was initially incarcerated, I had been charged with robbery, and my mother and landlord were going to post my bail – for robbery. Then two or three days later, my charges escalated from only robbery to robbery and murder; thus my bail was set at $200,000 which was beyond my mother's and landlord's financial ability to pay, so I remained in the county jail.

The crimes of robbery and murder had taken place on a Friday. I think that on the following Sunday after my co-defendant had learned that one of his victims had passed away, he may have gone to a friend's house in Canton, Ohio, because I think that this friend had previously somehow assisted my co-defendant before when my co-defendant had been "on the run." Then my co-defendant returned to the house in which we had been living. The landlord, who lived upstairs in the house in which this man, my two daughters, and I had been living heard someone in the house downstairs. I was the one who was renting that part of the house. The landlord knew that I was in jail and that my two daughters were staying at my parents' house, so the landlord called my mother who called the police. When the police reached the house, I assume that the landlord let them into the house. The police found my co-defendant lying on a bed with three or four guns around him and needles with which to shoot dope. He had never injected dope into his veins around me. I never saw him do that. When the police woke him up, he was in a daze. When they brought him out of the house, my young children and others were standing around watching. The police took him to the county jail.

That co-defendant publicly shamed me twice: once by involving me in his crimes and secondly by coming back to my house. He seemed to wear gloves a lot, probably to avoid leaving fingerprints since his fingerprints were in police data files because I learned later that he had been in and out of prison and had even escaped from a prison.

Some people, even today, when hearing about my co-defendant's crimes and my involvement as I have just related, criticize me for my actions then. Yes, I fully agree that I should not have obeyed my co-defendant's order for me to collect other people's money while they were held at gunpoint by my co-defendant and that I should not have driven the car away from the crimes that night when my co-defendant was in that car, and I should have notified the police of the crimes. However, some people say that she, meaning me, should not have done that or say something like, "I would have done this instead," or "I would not have done that," criticizing my behavior/misjudgments, but my response to people who say those things is that they are emotionally detached from that situation. Therefore, it is easy for these people to pass judgment on me, and looking back on an event(s), people have the luxury of knowing what the consequences or outcome of past actions were. Nevertheless, that night I was a part of the context of the situation. I was abruptly confronted with that situation and suddenly thrust into those circumstances, and it all happened so quickly. During that time period for me, I was terrified of this man. I frequently saw his gun where we lived, and he many times threatened me with it, telling me that he would kill my two precious, darling little daughters or me. And I didn't know just what to do about the circumstances then. I did try to get my daughters and me back into my parents' house to escape him. I guess the message I am trying to convey to disparagers is the adage, "until you walk the walk," you *really* don't know what you would do in a situation. Also, according to Christians of which I profess to be one, the Holy Bible states "for judgment belongs to God." I am also reminded of the incident recorded in the Christian Holy Bible when teachers and leaders of the law brought before Jesus a woman who had been caught in the act of adultery and told Jesus that according to the laws previously instructed by Moses that the consequence was for this woman to be stoned to death, and Jesus Christ said to them close to these words, "If anyone of you is without sin, let that person cast the first stone." As for my participation in my co-defendant's crimes, I was wrong, and unfortunately I learned the hard way, and believe me, I paid for it. From age twenty-seven years to forty-nine years, I was incarcerated.

For judgment belongs to God.

My Life Shattered

23

Chapter Five

My Legal Consequences

After the crimes of robbery and murder, considered as one crime, my co-defendant hid, but I was arrested a week later. Between the time of the murder and my arrest, I had started to come apart psychologically. At the time I was taken into custody, I was nervous, scared, and inexperienced in criminal affairs. I made a statement to the police that I did participate in the robbery. I must say I did walk out of a building with other people's money. However, although terrified of my co-defendant at the time, I did NOT know that he had planned to shoot anyone and I did NOT have a gun during the robbery. Two of the victims said that I had had a gun at the time, and two victims said that I did not have a gun then. All of the witnesses said that I was exiting the building or had already exited the building before my co-defendant shot and killed one of his victims.

My first lawyer told me to plead guilty to my co-defendant's crime of murder, and I thought, "Why should I plead guilty to something I didn't do? I wasn't even present when the murder occurred." After my co-defendant killed his victim, I did drive the car away, but at that time, I did not know that someone had gotten killed until the following Monday morning. My defense attorney stated that even though I might have been as much of a victim of my co-defendant (because of my fear of him) as a perpetrator, the lawyer told me that when someone is associated with a crime, the person who actually committed the crime and anyone associated with the criminal act is charged with the crime. Association was my situation and the situation of many of the other female inmates. The prosecutors believed that I was lying about me not knowing where my co-defendant was hiding. Since Ohio had recently before that reinstated the death penalty, the prosecutors threatened to ask for the death penalty for me if I went to trial and lost. If that would have occurred, I would have been the first woman in Ohio in modern times to get the death penalty.

Since I felt that I was psychologically fragile, I was examined by a psychologist, and against my belief, I was judged competent to stand trial. I ask rhetorically, while I was in the Justice Center, specifically I was in the mental ward and taking mind medication, so shouldn't this have been proof that at that time I was mentally unfit to stand trial? However, since I was judged competent to stand trial, at my lawyer's advice, on June 2, 1982, I plea bargained complicity and had no jury trial. I pled guilty to simple murder and two counts of aggravated robbery, and the aggravated burglary and aggravated murder charges were dropped.

Originally I had agreed to testify at my co-defendant's trial but before his trial, I changed my mind because at the time, in my weak mental state, I felt that I was just too terrified of my co-defendant to face him in court, plus I had not witnessed the murder anyway, so I thought that my testimony about the murder would have been pointless. My last minute reluctance to testify against my co-defendant angered the prosecuting attorneys; they did not believe that my mental state was in such a "shaky" state.

For the murder charge, I received a fifteen-year-to-life prison sentence, and for the two robbery charges, I received two seven-to-twenty-five year sentences to run concurrently except one of the sentences. My total prison sentence was twenty-two years to life. Convicted criminals do serve prison time as long as the prison sentence states. My lawyers then told me that with good behavior, I would be out of prison in fourteen years. However, as it turned out, I was in prison for twenty-two years. In hindsight, I probably would have received a shorter sentence if I had had a jury trial. My co-defendant's trial resulted in him receiving a thirty-year-to-life prison sentence. At this writing, he is still incarcerated.

Facing my prison sentence, I had one comfort, that being that my exceedingly gracious, precious parents were going to take custody of my two darling daughters. Therefore, I knew that my cherished children would be well taken care of and raised well, and both of them could stay together instead of the possibility of them being put into separate foster homes.

Chapter Six

Prison Life

I spent a total of twenty-two years in prison, ten years in Marysville Reformatory For Women in Marysville, Ohio, and twelve years in the Northeast Pre-Release Center in Cleveland, Ohio. I entered prison to serve my prison sentence when I was twenty-seven years of age and was released from prison at age forty-nine years, from 1982 to 2003. Specifically, I was sentenced on October 21, 1982, and actually entered prison on November 4, 1982. I was released from prison on October 6, 2003.

Having gone into prison when I was twenty-seven years old, there were younger people than me working there, prison officials called COs, who were giving me orders, telling me what to do, like every little thing. I thought to myself, "This isn't going to work."

In addition, for women who like to wear false hair or false fingernails, these women can forget about all of that because it will all come off. Prison officials, or should I say the way the "system" works, they want inmates to look and feel as rough and as ugly as possible.

When I first got into prison, I used to sit back and observe people and things to see ways I thought that I could possibly escape, like everybody else. I thought if I'm going to do fifteen to twenty years, what do I have to lose? But then I thought that if I ran, I might never see my children again, and I couldn't talk with them without looking over my shoulder for the police, and I didn't want my children to have that fear or put them into any kind of jeopardy. While in prison, sometimes I'd think about killing myself, just not wake up. I thought that I didn't even care anymore. I shouldn't have thought that way. I guess when a person is in

27

a place like that, many thoughts go through that person's mind.

When I entered Marysville Prison, at that time there were three hundred women incarcerated there, and amazingly there were no confining fences. The prison was located in a very rural area with much sprawling land like farms surrounding it. Chickens, cows, and other farm animals were right on the prison grounds. Inmates and prison employees could hear cows mooing throughout the days and nights, and sometimes a rooster's crowing would wake a person up in the mornings. Having been raised on a farm, I was not particularly bothered by these animal noises, but I think that some of the other inmates were.

When a prisoner was discovered to have escaped, a loud whistle would blow three times. One long whistle blow signaled a capture. Eventually, fences were erected to encompass Marysville prison and stricter rules were created.

Marysville prison opened in 1916 when thirty-four female inmates from the Ohio Penitentiary in Columbus, Ohio, were transferred there. I was told about a part of the prison where at least some prison inmates of long ago had probably been kept. One could still see the chains and shackles of restraint attached to the old stone walls of this dreadful, dark, dingy dungeon. According to an inmate, that hellish "pit" was still used at times for exceptionally difficult-to-manage prisoners, sometimes never to be seen again. According to a supposed observer, the sign of the devil was sprawled on one of the walls of this horrid place. I remember that once I passed by this awful part of the prison when its door leading down those dark, old, creepy steps was open. I got an eerie feeling and knew that I wanted no part of that area.

In modern times when I was incarcerated, I observed that some inmates did try to kill themselves. There were many disturbed inmates. I think many of them were disturbed before they came to prison. These people were a main reason why prison was such a dangerous place. An inmate had to worry and watch out being around people like that. For example, another inmate could be a psychopath who may appear "normal" on the outside and unexpectedly do something harmful to another inmate. For instance, an inmate could go to sleep not knowing what a disturbed inmate might do to the sleeping inmate. I saw people beaten. Sometimes an inmate would put a combination lock into a sock and then beat another inmate with this weapon. I saw hot coffee thrown into other people's faces. I did not know them, but I saw some of the famed cultist killer, Charles Manson's, followers while in prison. You never knew what another person was thinking. Prison was a scary place. You had to keep your guard up because you didn't know who you could really trust.

As for people on the outside of prison, when a person goes to prison, that is when she/he finds out who her/his friends really are. When a person is incarcerated, that is when the inmate discovers who truly loves her/him. Many people on the outside of prison do not want to be bothered with people who are in prison. They think that the inmate will always want something or is deranged. If a person had friends before entering prison, once that person becomes incarcerated, these friends soon fade away which really creates a hurtful feeling for the inmate.

When I was in the county jail, I soon learned that I had an additional situation to deal with; I was unknowingly pregnant with a third child by my co-defendant. I was then taken to Metro Hospital where I was given psychiatric drugs and put onto suicide watch when I was first arrested. When I was in the county jail, I was removed from the floor that I had been on and taken to the mental ward until I was transferred to Marysville Prison. I had been sent to prison in that condition. When medical people, prison officials and I discovered my pregnancy, I was immediately taken off those psychiatric drugs.

Next I was put into the Marysville Hospital for the remainder of my pregnancy. I wondered how I could be or feel like a surrogate mother for my three children. I questioned the authenticity of the doctors and nurses in this prison hospital. To me, they appeared to be just playing those roles. When it was apparent that I was about to give birth, I told the prison medical people that I wanted to have my child in an actual hospital. A nurse at the prison hospital said to me, "OH, it's nothing; you're not ready." I retorted, "I am ready NOW!" Although I was eventually taken to Memorial Hospital, the doctors there were very angry with the prison officials for waiting so long. The unnecessary delay could have seriously endangered my baby. Fortunately though, by the grace of God, my baby was fine.

After I had my baby girl, I spent around two days in an isolated cell in Memorial Hospital in Columbus, Ohio. All prisoners are put into a holding part of the hospital because they are inmates. When an inmate was away from Marysville Prison, the inmate was always kept completely away from people on the street to reduce or hopefully eliminate the possibility of the inmate escaping or causing any other unwanted event. Then I was taken back to Marysville Prison. My baby was put into the prison's nursery center. "High status" prison inmates cared for other inmates' babies until the babies were picked up by a family member(s). Everyday a nurse brought my baby to me in my room for one half to one hour in the Marysville hospital. This practice allowed the mother to get to know her baby and could feed her infant. This procedure was followed while awaiting the completion of paperwork for my mother to come and take my baby. This was a very lonely time for me. One day when my child was brought to me and we were customarily locked in the room, I picked up my baby's gown and discovered four marks on my baby's legs. I pounded on the cell door and demanded to know what had happened to my precious little baby. A nurse came and took my baby, and prison officials started an investigation to discover what had happened.

The result of the investigation disgusted me. The marks turned out to be burn marks, and I was falsely accused of doing it! It seemed to me that prison officials were quick to blame an inmate with a murder and robbery record. I think that the burn marks on my baby was the first such case. While I was in the warden's office with the deputy sheriff and state troopers who were trying to get me to sign a paper to put my child up for adoption, my room was being "shaken down". At that time, I was allowed to smoke, so I had cigarettes and matches in my room. Prison personnel tried to tell me that because my co-defendant got me pregnant and association with his committed crime put me into prison that I was taking out my anger on my baby. How absurd and wrong they were! Perhaps these medical people try to use their psychology by trying to fit people into categories. So much for their assessment. At this time I was not on any mind medication because I was pregnant, so my mind was clear, and I argued on my behalf. After that, I did not see my baby because prison officials stopped me from seeing my daughter. I was so very distraught! I didn't know where my baby was! Prison officials were scanning everything and would not let me send a letter out, so I got some kind, anonymous other inmate who worked in the prison hospital to mail a letter to my mother for me in which I told my mother to hurry to the prison as soon as possible to get my baby because I was in serious jeopardy of losing my adored child. Prison officials tried to get me to sign a paper to give my baby up for adoption because of the sentence I had, but I wouldn't sign. I angrily said to them, "When my parents get here, we'll sign a whole bunch of papers, and I'll sue you!" Then I was given psychological tests and over medicated to the point that I couldn't even read a clock! I had a complete nervous breakdown. Prison officials had me so medicated and prevented me from   seeing my daughter. All I could do was to sit in my cell and worry day and night.

All of this time, I was not allowed to be out of my room. My door stayed locked and was open only to receive mail, my food tray, and medication.

Being locked in a medical unit in the prison hospital, when prison guards opened the door, I pushed to get out to see my baby; buttons were pressed, and a multitude of guards in riot gear came running toward me, and following a physical altercation, I was overwhelmed and subdued and put back into the room. They did not like the fact that I wanted to see where my daughter was. I did not know where my daughter was at that time. I just didn't know.

Then came the reckoning; my parents, one of my sisters, and a friend showed up! A vehement argument in the warden's office ensued. My mother looked directly into the warden's eyes and firmly declared, "I'm Marilyn's mother, and I'm taking the baby. Marilyn sent me a letter and said she didn't hurt her baby. Marilyn would never harm her children. There are no doctors' reports or any other records that show that she has ever hurt her other two daughters when she was home with them before she went to prison."

Finally I was led to a door and I knew that the plight of my baby lie on the other side of that ominous door. No one had told me anything. I thought, "What scene will I see on the other side of that door? Will I see a social worker taking my dear baby away? Will this be the last time I will ever see my baby?" Every fiber in my being tightened up, and I shook; however, I knew even stronger was my desire to see what was happening and who I would see on the other side of that cold, steel door. I wanted and needed to know. I pushed open the door, and to my unexplainable joy I saw my wonderful, dear mother there to take my baby home. I cried tears of happiness! My mother took my youngest daughter home, so now I knew that my baby would be well taken care of, and I did not lose my child. Now I had three lovely daughters.

The battle for myself with the long prison sentence

combined with the fight for my youngest child had its consequences though. I suffered a nervous breakdown. I was then taken to a kangaroo court. This is a court that is held in a prison with a real judge who had read papers to see if I was mentally ill. I was not sure where this judge came from, but he had to evaluate me to see if I was mentally ill. He saw the condition I was in, and I was trying to explain what had happened to me because at this point, no one knew what had really happened with my child. I am sure that this judge read what prison officials had written about me. Thus, at this point, the judge declared me to be insane, so I was sent to The Timothy B. Moritz Forensic Center for the criminally insane. I was mentally deranged. I stayed there for six months before I was sent back to the Ohio Reformatory For Women to finish my life sentence. The officials in the Forensic Center would evaluate a person every three months. There I was seen by some other doctors who I thought were "crazier" than I, and I was placed on more medications for my mind. At The Timothy B. Moritz Forensic Center, I really cannot feel how prison officials thought I was supposed to handle a charge of murder which I didn't commit, face a twenty-two-year prison sentence, and having my daughter burned in the prison. All of these mental stressors were present before I left the court, but I had not hurt my baby.

What should have been done when I was going to trial was to have been sent to the Forensic Center while I was in the Justice Center to see if I was mentally competent to go to court to stand trial for my case before I was sentenced. At the Justice Center a doctor said that I was competent to stand trial when I wasn't. This problem lingered through my stays at the Justice Center and Marysville, and my battles for my baby and for myself worsened my condition until I had a nervous breakdown.

Now, a person is examined in a forensic center and if proclaimed competent, then the person is returned to the

Justice Center and stands trial. I felt that the constitutional rights of my daughter and myself were violated through this whole ordeal. The fact that the doctor in the Justice Center said that I was competent but I was not because as soon as I went to Marysville, I gave birth and because I could have gotten the electric chair plus I was not competent. I had a complete nervous breakdown. Since I had had no dealings with the law previously, I was unfamiliar with it, so I was exceedingly scared.

Later when I went out into the general prison population, some of the other inmates would say, "That's the woman who hurt her baby." I was so humiliated by this unwarranted stigma. Also, I felt that my rights had been violated by the prison officials because a prison official told me that my daughter had a staph infection, which turned out be a lie.

In my opinion, I do not think that the prison inmates who took care of the babies were good, and the prison officials appeared to me to be in a big hurry to just "write my case off." Also, just for the sake of knowing, another baby had burn marks, so prison officials eventually discovered that a prison inmate who was watching the children in the prison daycare center was the culprit who had burned my dear baby's legs. At first they said that I had burned my daughter, and then they said she had a staph infection until the second baby was burned.

I kept saying that I had been abused by my co-defendant, but no one recognized it until ten+ years later. Hundreds of inmates had been abused but were ashamed to admit it. During my incarceration, I attended a workshop on domestic violence. While there listening, I began relating what I was hearing to my own situation while I was living with my co-defendant. Thus while in prison, I read all of the papers that there were about abuse, and a "bell went off" in my head. I thought to myself, "I had been abused by this man," my co-defendant. Back then, domestic violence was not as publicly discussed. I don't think that an average person knew anything about it or possibly knew just a little about it. I think that domestic violence can and does also occur to White women living in affluent areas, not just to Black women and/or in economically poor neighborhoods. Every woman wants to cover up domestic violence because of the time and effort that she has exerted in the relationship. But I think, why stay in an abusive relationship?

As for the guards, there were both women and men guards. I thought that generally the guards in Marysville were more "straight-laced" and adhered strictly to the book whereas the guards at the Northeast Pre-Release Center seemed to me to be more "down-to-earth". As in many areas in life, there were occasional cover ups. Some people got caught and some did not. Some of the inmates had babies from some of the guards. Also, I saw several people pass away in prison, having medical concerns; I suppose inmates passing away replicated the "outside" general population. Even though I had had mental issues and had given birth to a child, I had no physically-oriented medical problems until I got home, and I'm glad that I was home by that time. However, I personally never thought I'd ever make it out of prison alive. I used to pray to God to not let me die in this place. Sometimes I would read in The Holy Bible Psalms 23 and 83 to pick me up when I was very depressed while in prison. I know that God gave me the needed strength.

During my time in prison, I saw many inmates be released and return for crimes they had committed after they had been out of prison, some of the same people coming in and out, in and out, like they were in a revolving door. Also, many women in prison were there not because of what they had done but because of implication/association with their men who were the ones who had actually committed the crimes. In addition, after many inmates' sentences were completed, these inmates went home with medical problems. For example, recommended routine tests like pap smears were not done because it cost $3.00 to see a doctor for any reason. That amount was a large percentage of money in an inmate's account, so for example, if an inmate had a lump somewhere, the inmate could probably have had it checked out by the medical staff, but some women had no money or so little money, like maybe $10.00, in their accounts, that they did not go to the medical staff. Thus, medical conditions that could have possibly been detected in their early stages worsened because of the inmate's lack of finances. Everyone received state pay, but everyone knew that if an inmate visited a doctor for any reason, it would cost the inmate $3.00. Some inmates would just live off their state pay. If one of those inmates went to a doctor but did not have the required money, when that inmate received her state pay, the monetary cost of seeing the doctor was automatically deducted from the financial amount that the inmate received from the state.

For incoming personal mail, someone would stop by with a bucket containing letters received for inmates. Inmates would gather around and the names on the letter envelopes would be read. When a name was called, that inmate would step up and take the letter. Prison officials would open each envelope before it was given to each unit to be sure that the contents contained no contraband, but the prison officials did not read the letters unless an inmate was under investigation. However, when an inmate received a legal letter such as a letter from an inmate's lawyer, the inmate had to go to the prison's mailroom and sign for the letter. Like personal mail, the envelopes containing legal contents were opened just to verify there was no contraband, but the contents were not read by legal officials unless the inmate was presently under investigation for something. The difference was that the envelopes containing legal contents could not be opened by prison officials without the inmate being present. If prison officials saw a money order in the envelope, they processed it and put it onto the inmate's account. The inmate was then given an envelope stating the amount of the money order.

The prison commissary was a store where inmates could shop once a week; inmates could purchase items there but could not actually enter it, the back where the products were. Interested inmates wrote on the commissary list, listing available items, and the inmates would write how many of whatever item(s) they wanted to purchase. A commissary worker would bring the item(s) to the front, and staff at the commissary would add up the purchase. The inmate would then step to the window and sign for the items. At the NEPRC, different units got different days to shop which was once a week.

It was expensive to live in prison. No matter how much money an inmate had, there was a $50.00 per week maximum for total expenditures which did not affect those inmates who had no or little money, but inmates who received money orders from people outside of prison had this limit. Inmates had to buy items, usually personals, in the store. Most of the inmates bought canned goods. I particularly liked ice cream but when I bought some, I had to consume it immediately since inmates had no refrigerators or freezers in which to store ice cream. For awhile I lived in a prison version of a dormitory housing four to six inmates. Each inmate had a container like an army box that could be locked. Inmates stored their possessions in these boxes. Depending on who your roommate was, a prudent inmate would keep her container locked or unlocked. Maybe if an inmate wouldn't have money, she would steal deodorant, lotion, food or whatever from another inmate's personal locker. This caused a lot of fights. When I first got to prison, an inmate was given deodorant and other personal items, and maybe eventually an inmate could get items like personal soap, deodorant, etc. from the chaplain, but many fights occurred between/among prison roommates because someone would not have something and then she did, so another inmate would know that the inmate with the item had stolen it from her. For part of my prison term, I had only a few other cell inmates who were "cool" so I didn't have to lock my locker. In the "Honor Dorm," next to my cell was another cell with two other inmates. The four of us shared the hallway and shower/washroom. This arrangement was considered an honor room. Inmates who occupied this room had to be inmates who had good behavior, had no "tickets". A "ticket" was an undesirable item to get. It was a result of something an inmate did that broke a prison rule. The result would be temporary restrictions such as possibly limited telephone use or no telephone use at all for a specified length of time or an "early to bed" restraint, or some other limit as a form of punishment.

Inmates don't just sit around all day; they work. Everyone in prison had to work. Prison officials tried to assign a job that was appropriate to an inmate's background. If an inmate returned to prison, that inmate was given a nastier job such as working in the kitchen. The top pay was probably $18.00 to $20.00 a month, depending on the job. The highest-paying job was making flags. Personally, I did laundry. The amounts of money that inmates earned from their prison jobs were not enough for inmates to financially survive. Inmates needed additional money coming in such as from family. An inmate's family could send any amount of money to the inmate. The only way that an inmate would not have to work was if the inmate was non-functional, and that person would live in the prison hospital. For inmates who had very low IQs, they had to go to school instead of work. If someone refused to work, that inmate was sent to the hole for maybe fifteen days. After emerging from the hole, the inmate was usually willing to comply by working.

Nearly everything in prison was continuously monitored. Even the number of articles of clothing was known, clothing sent from home plus state clothes. Each unit had a microwave oven, an iron, a workout area among other daily common maintenance items. There was a microwave oven that inmates could use, but it was next to a guard's desk so that the microwave use could be closely supervised. There were three prisoner counts per day to indicate to prison officials if a prisoner(s) had escaped. When a new shift of prison employees started, there was a prisoner count at 6:30 a.m. After this count was taken, prison inmates could go to breakfast. Afterwards was my shift in the laundry room. Then there was another prisoner count at 9:00 p.m. After that calculation was made, a prison inmate could come out of her cell or remain in her room. Then the day's final prisoner count came at 11:30 p.m. after which prison inmates had to remain in their cells except any inmates who had some nighttime jobs in their units.

IDs were VERY IMPORTANT in prison. Whenever an inmate left her room, she had to have her ID on ANYTHING she wore even if a guard knew who she was. It didn't make a difference where the inmate went outside of her cell, whether it was to the day room or ironing board; she had to display her ID. A lost or damaged identification badge had to be replaced and paid for by the inmate, and no stickers, tags, pins, and the like could ever be on the badge. There was no loitering permitted around the basketball court, certain walkways or other units, when inmates' visitors were entering and exiting the premises, and where and when Parole Board Hearings were being held. An inmate could not go into another unit without permission. When laundry was submitted for cleaning, the inmate had to complete an itemized list. Then when the laundry was returned, in the presence of a laundry worker or correction officer, the inmate had to sign the sheet of paper confirming that all items were present. The only privacy afforded inmates was a washroom. If inmates wanted to engage in sexual activity, they would do so wherever they could find a spot where a camera was not there or where there were no people.

39

Sometimes they would have another inmate be a lookout, watching for guards. Some female inmates did not like other inmates, but many of them did have other female inmates as lovers.

In addition to legal assistance, more personally, family support is extremely fantastic. Throughout my incarceration, I had strong family support. I must say that I never wanted for anything. Because I had been locked up for a long time, at that time, these inmates, including me, could have items that were not generally considered inmate garb. Sometimes I even wore high heeled shoes in prison! My family never complained about telephone bills. I could call them anytime. And probably the most important benefit to the superb family support I received was that maintaining those close family ties enabled me to not lose my sanity. Prison is a very lonely place in which to be. When my children were very young, my loving, insightful parents would bring my precious children to visit me when I was in prison. My parents were also generous by occasionally giving me money. They would put money into my account. Then when my children became adults, they periodically presented me with food, clothing, and money. My children financially took care of me. Also, my sister, Mary, was exceptionally good to me when I was in prison. She was a sweetheart, sending me food boxes and clothes. Generally, my brothers and sisters did not visit me when I was in prison. Although I did have financial assistance from some of my exceedingly loving family members, sometimes I would play games over the telephone to get extra money. I must admit that at times I baited men by talking sex with them over the telephone to get them to send me money as my earnings for prison work amounted to a maximum of $19.00 per month. Some female inmate might want another inmate to talk with some guy, and she would tell him what he wanted to hear, and he would think that she was ready to get out of prison. Some of these men were extremely naughty. The bottom line was that these men were freaky. Then she would tell him to send to her a money order. The woman inmate would get his contact information and then send him a letter telling him to put the mother's, father's, sister's or brother's name on the money order, and the inmate would get the money. In prison, if a person was not on an inmate's visiting list, that inmate was not allowed to receive a money order from that person. As financially broke as some inmates were, I wonder why that would matter.

I was blessed to have people on the outside who cared about what happened to me and was also fortunate for having a good friend on the inside, my wonderful friend, Carmen Williams. It's hard to live in prison. An inmate needs to have money and friends. Carmen went to prison when she was seventeen years old and was already in prison when I arrived there. According to Carmen, the first time she saw me was at the Central Food Service in Marysville prison. One of Carmen's dreams before she had become incarcerated was to become a model. Possibly that is what had attracted her to me when she saw me as she thought that I was attractive-looking and that she thought that I looked so sad. I was pregnant at that time, and when most women are pregnant to where they are showing, they don't feel like they look good, so I guess at that time, to have someone else think I looked nice made me feel better about myself. During this time when I was generally feeling unhappy, Carmen was the only person who used to frequently come to see me. I appreciated that. Over time, the more Carmen and I talked with each other, the more we learned how many things we had in common. Before our incarcerations, we had some of the same goals in life, those dreams being shattered by our plight of incarceration. She and I had both been, separately, charged with robbery and murder although neither of us were actually present during the murders with which she and I had been associated. To reiterate, the incidents that caused Carmen and me to land in prison were completely unrelated. At the time that her incident occurred and my situation happened, Carmen and I did not even know each other then. Our criminal sentences were very similar; she was doomed to prison for the rest of her natural life and the death sentence of which fortunately never occurred. While Carmen was imprisoned, concerning the criminal act with which she had been charged, she was reclassified as an accessory to murder.

Carmen Williams- My Most Valued Friend

She really helped me become acclimated to prison life and greatly helped me serve my prison sentence. We were in Marysville at the same time and later were roommates in the NEPRC. What happened to Carmen was tragic for her. My dream while in prison was to come home and be with my children and my parents while they were still in this world because many inmates went to funerals during their time in prison. When I was in prison and an inmate's immediate family member passed away, that inmate, dressed in an orange jumpsuit and handcuffed, was allowed to visit the family member's remains at a funeral parlor accompanied by two guards. The inmate was taken to the funeral parlor when no other visitors were there and was allowed to stay there for a half an hour or an hour and was then brought back to the prison. If the inmate did not have an escape record, that inmate could go, but first, that inmate's family would have to send some money to pay for the prison guard escort. Over the years of my incarceration, I saw many inmates returning from funeral parlors, and the inmates looked so distraught. I could see the deep sadness and acute pain on their faces. I prayed to God that I would never have a reason to visit a funeral parlor during the years of my incarceration. I used to pray to God to keep my family members alive while I was in prison. I did not want to go to any funerals while I was in prison. I know that God answers prayer because He answered my prayer. That is a huge prayer that our dear God answered for me because a family member's passing away when I was in prison would have been very difficult to deal with. It was hard enough just being away from my family. Fortunately, my parents remained in this world longer than my imprisonment. My father lived in this world for three years after I got out of prison and passed away from heart problems while practically in my arms. My mother lived in this world for seven years after, passing away ultimately from lung cancer. However, my good friend, Carmen, was not that fortunate.

During Carmen's imprisonment in The Northeast Pre-Release Center, her precious mother passed away from cancer. Carmen was unspeakably grief-stricken as she had been close to her mother. Carmen became distant from me like she was in a world of her own. Then, unbeknownst to me, Carmen and another inmate planned and accomplished an escape from The Northeast Pre-Release Center with the help of a staff member. She wanted to see her family. Carmen and the other inmate were eventually captured and brought back to prison.

One day Carmen asked me, "Marilyn, what would you think about having a cancer walk-a-thon?" I replied, "Sounds great to me." Carmen then asked me, "Would you help me put it on?" I said, "Sure." She wanted to do a cancer walk-a-thon because her mother had passed away from this dreaded illness. Carmen was uncertain how this walk-a-thon would be received, thinking that possibly most people would take the situation for granted. However, together we created and executed a cancer walk-a-thon, successfully raising $1,000 for the cause. The event was covered in *The Plain Dealer* newspaper, the October 24, 1993 issue. This walk-a-thon continues to this day at The Northeast Pre-Release Center. In fact, in 2012 the inmates there raised over $4,000. However, Carmen and I exceedingly want to be recognized as the founders of this walk-a-thon, and Carmen would fervently like for her mother, Ms. Annastean D. Roper, to be recognized by name as the reason for the creation of this cancer walk-a-thon. However, unfortunately Carmen and I seem to have faded from the minds of the subsequent leaders of this cancer walk-a-thon. To the best of our knowledge, Carmen and I are not mentioned when this walk-a-thon occurs annually. Realistically, that annual event would not exist if it had not been for Carmen. Also, in my later prison years, after a screening of the film, *Songbirds*, part of the Cleveland, Ohio, International Film Festival, I was a member of the panel group, "Talkback," a fundraiser for the

Women's Community Foundation, that discussed the film. While I was still incarcerated, another program in which I was involved was the prison's "Scared Straight" program, a program in which some episodes filmed at other prisons are occasionally broadcast over televisions.

The two biggest challenges of being in prison are dealing with the loss of freedom and loneliness. Nearly everything in prison was continuously monitored. Even the number of articles of clothing for each inmate was known. There was a microwave oven that inmates could use, but it was next to a guard's desk so that the microwave use could be closely supervised. Also, there were rules; for example, a lost or damaged identification badge had to be replaced and paid for by the inmate, and no stickers, tags, pins, and the like could be on the badge. Having an identification badge in prison was absolutely necessary. There was no loitering permitted around the basketball court, certain walkways, when inmates' visitors were entering and exiting the premises, and where and when Parole Board Hearings were being held. When laundry was submitted for cleaning, the inmate had to complete an itemized list. Then when the laundry was returned in the presence of a laundry worker or correction officer confirming that all items were present, the inmate had to sign the sheet of paper containing the list.

The food service at the NEPRC also had its constraints. When working or coming to eat at the food service area, all inmates were to adhere to appropriate behavior which meant no loud talking, no use of profanity, and no talking across the serving line. No radios, books, or playing cards were ever permitted in the food service area. The inmates were counted before each of the three daily meals. The food service area was open for one hour for each meal. For daily dinner, weekly sanitation ratings determined the order in which inmates of various housing units were called. The mess hall was not very big; maybe three units would eat there and then another unit or two would go there. No food was to leave the food service area. Food had to be eaten there. However, there would not have been much to take out anyway because the food portions were like for seven or eight-year-olds. The only times inmates were given big portions were like on Thanksgiving Day and Christmas. We ate breakfast early in the morning, lunch, and then dinner around 4:00 p.m., but what about the rest of the evening? Many of us inmates became hungry during some evenings. If an inmate was hungry and had no money in her account, she remained hungry for the rest of the evening unless someone would lend the hungry person something. Some people would give freely like a cupcake or something, and some people were stingy. If someone was a diabetic, she could get something to eat, a snack, through nurses, in the evening. I do not think that we were fed well in prison. Very fortunate for me, I never worried about that because my parents always made sure I had money in my account, and when my children were young, my parents would bring them to see me. Then when my children became adults, they would give me money and boxes of clothes. I felt really good that my children continued to love me during the twenty-two years that I was imprisoned. I thought that maybe I had lost their love forever, but I had not. During my incarceration, my youngest daughter, Khaleedah, wrote me this sensational poem:

A Daughter's Love

Where were you, Mama?
Do you realize I went through some drama?
Why weren't you here?
Or did you not know how to stoor?
Can you understand
Why I'm not one of your biggest fans?
Do you think this is a race
Or are you going to go at my pace?
Do you even have a clue
What hell I've been through
Without having you?
Can't you understand
Why we don't walk hand and hand?
Mom, I love you
But I still don't think you have a clue..
I will continue to stay strong
Because I know I did nothing wrong.
I am not angry.
I am not even sad,
But there are some things I wish I had.
Mentally, you weren't there..
Physically, you are still not here..
Emotionally, I know you care..
You are not only a friend; you're my mother.
I'm not only your daughter; I'm also your other.
Mom, I know you fell the loops.
It's time you get back up and go through the hoops.
I am bound
To keep my feet firmly on the ground.

47

I stand tall
To rise and soar above all.
I keep my head up
Because I am tired of being fed up.
I have courage
So no one can make me discouraged.
I can say I'm like a piece of clay
Because you told me
I mold me.
And no one can scold me..
I know I am a diamond
Because I will always shine..
But you don't have to believe now.
You will see in time,
Sometimes I may need polish,
But remember one thing,
I will never be abolished.
Mom I will always be there
Because I am your other, daughter, and your friend,
And I truly care.

I was really awestruck after I read my precious daughter's poem.

Khaleedah

Notwithstanding though, returning to another example of a set of rules dealt with the commissary where inmates could purchase items. Inmates were allowed to shop once per week with a maximum total purchase(s) of $50.00 excluding appliances. If an inmate went over the $50.00 maximum, the inmate would have to put something back. The order of shopping by unit was based on the cleanliness of the units, meaning that the inmates with the cleanest unit shopped first and so on. The advantage of having a clean unit which led to the order in which inmates did their shopping was that those inmates who shopped first had a better chance of being able to buy what they wanted before the stock became depleted. By the time some of the inmates attempted to buy an item, that item had already been sold out. Inmates called to the commissary to pick up their orders were called in groups of fifteen. We had to remain inside of glass double doors or outside until we were called to the commissary window. Only one inmate at a time was allowed at the window and had to conduct herself in a quiet and orderly fashion.

At the NEPRC, all of the people on all inmates' visitors' lists had to be "verified" before the visitor(s) could gain entry to visit the inmate that he or she had come to visit. "Verification" applied to EVERYONE – relatives, friends, people who sent money to inmates, etc. To become "verified," a prospective visitor had to provide identity by producing to appropriate prison officials a birth certificate, marriage certificate, etc., complete a visitor application, and be interviewed at the prison. It was the inmates' responsibility to make sure that any visitors were verified. The prison officials were very strict in adhering to the rule that no one could be placed on a visitor's list who had been in prison unless that person could produce a legal document stating that that former prison inmate was no longer on parole or probation.

However, there were some positive aspects of prison.

The NEPRC offered programs in obtaining a GED, domestic violence classes, computer classes, aggression control, regaining values, freedom from smoking, parenting plus, chronic pain management, expressive art therapy, a pet program of blind people, diversity and cultural awareness. For a time, in Marysville, an inmate could take college courses toward a college degree. Religious worship services and Bible studies were offered. The NEPRC had two libraries; one was for more leisure reading of newer fiction, non-fiction, references, newspapers and magazines. The other library was a law library which could assist inmates with child custody issues, guardianship authorization/Power of Attorney, Felony Overriding Misdemeanor Cases, and Jail-Time Credit, among other issues. There was also a notary available at various times. Also, an inmate's family could place an order for a specific magazine, but the magazine itself had to come directly from its publisher. My view was that I had the time, so I took advantage of some of the prison offerings to better myself. Specifically, the programs that I completed while in prison were co-dependency, cancer walk-a-thon project, earned a Templum House Domestic Violence certificate, Current Events certificate, GED, stress management certificate, juvenile court project, assertiveness certificate, keyboarding certificate, Laubach Literacy Program, Community Re-entry Program, evaluation report from Ms. McGuire for the cancer walk-a-thon, attended Urbana College for three quarters for a Liberal Arts degree, earned a cosmetology license as an operator, manager, and instructor, Greater Cleveland Growth association Project, National Clearing House for the Defense of Battered Women Project, Alcoholics Anonymous meetings, and community hours/car wash. I also spent much time in the law library trying to find a way out of prison.

At Marysville Prison, other availabilities included a guidance counselor who rendered help with keeping an inmate's educational file current, correctly completing an inmate's class interest checklist, taking GED and other tests, and checking on a high school or GED transcript. While I was in prison, I took advantage of educational opportunities afforded me. I studied for the GED, the equivalent of a high school diploma, and kept taking it until I passed it. I took the GED test seven times until I obtained it. Then I started a college program while in Marysville Prison. That opportunity was eventually stopped because some people complained that inmates were in college, and these people said that they had to send their children to college, thus the situation being unfair. Thus, there was not a college option at The Northeast Pre-Release Center. However, while I was incarcerated in The Northeast Pre-Release Center, I also earned a cosmetology license, and still as a prison inmate, I became a cosmetology instructor and manager of that prison's cosmetology center. In Marysville Prison, I earned a hair styling license and worked doing staff and inmates' hair. At Marysville Prison, I worked in the Prison's salon working with my instructors. Later at the Northeast Pre-Release Center, I was the manager of the prison hair salon. I ran that salon myself.

The mental health department provided psychiatric, psychological, and social services. Available programs were Stress Management, Medication Education, Anger Management, Depression, and Coping. Many of these offerings were in Marysville Prison whereas in the NEPRC, there was a group of professionals in these areas that inmates could contact for help once the inmates were released from prison.

There was also a recreation department and arts and crafts center. Some of those options were painting, needlepoint, making cards, and making clothes which had to be sent home. In the NEPRC, there was a talent show that I was in every month. I loved singing to the crowd of women. I felt free during those times.

Regarding the prisons' regulations, when I was

younger, I didn't want anyone telling me anything. Then for twenty-two years people were telling me what to do. I must state, though, that I will never again try to get myself caught up as I did previously; the consequences were terrifying, but I learned a lesson – live life straightly.

Sometimes if a person first came into prison and was depressed, since I had been in prison for a long time, sometimes guards would ask me to talk with the person. Many inmates were there for the first time, and they were scared being away from home, having no family there. When I entered prison, I was extremely scared, and it took me awhile to adjust to being in prison. After being there for a long time, when asked to talk with some of the new arrivals, I would tell the person that it's not so bad and that before she knew it, her time in prison would be up. I'd say that I'd been in prison for twenty years, so she could do her one year and that I didn't know when it will be up for me. Some of these women would say to me, "How could you do twenty-two years?" I'd say that God gave me the strength, and I thought the rest came from me. I'd tell myself that I have to do this. I made a lot of people feel better in prison. It did not matter to me if these people were Black or White; we were all sisters in the same "boat".

Some movies like the *Shawshank Redemption* although the stories are fictionalized, very closely resemble how prison life is in men's prisons, how men are treated and the gangs, but there are incidences that occur in women's prisons. There are crooked guards everywhere. Sometimes inmates fight between and among themselves but not as much as in men's prisons. There were a lot of killings and beatings going on in prison, so the average inmate really had to watch her back in prison so that no one would "set her up," putting her in the middle of some situation. Also, there were cover-ups. In addition, there is some lesbian-type behavior in women's prisons. I think that some women would most likely be lesbians whether they were in or out of prison, being lesbians "on the street," but there is a significant number of female inmates who engage in lesbianism while in prison who probably would not get involved in that behavior if they were not incarcerated, but in prison female-to-female encounters occasionally happen out of a sense of emotional survival. There were many women who did not engage in lesbianism. Conversely, some of the guards were lesbians.

To sum up prison life in general, I would say that prison is like a world of its own, a place that I NEVER want to be in again. Prison is somewhat like depictions of it in some movies, and only the strong survive that place. It is a severe nightmare, a place where no one wants to ever be. And once a person has been in prison, that person is scarred for the rest of his or her life. That prison record in a person's past most of the time prevents the person from obtaining quality employment for the rest of his or her life. So take it from me, stay out of prison if you can. If for some reason(s) you end up committing some crime, at least try to not get caught.

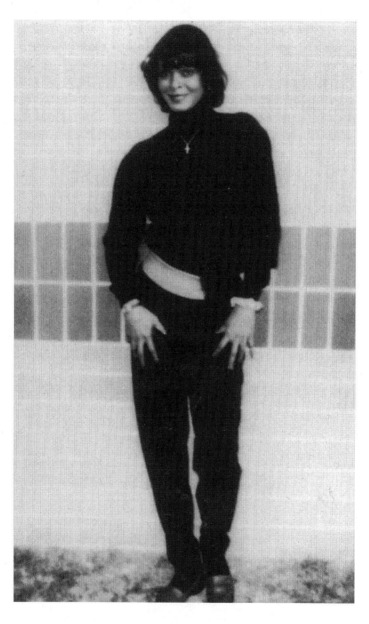

Still Being Fashionable Within The Walls

Stay out of prison
if you can.

ELIZABETH KELLEY L.P.A. INC.

800 STANDARD BUILDING
1370 ONTARIO STREET
CLEVELAND, OHIO 44113
TELEPHONE (216) 523-1113
FAX (216) 621-0575
EMAIL ekelley@ald.net

November 18, 2001

Marilyn Lowery
15896
Unit J
Northeast Pre-Release Center
2675 East 30th Street
Cleveland, Ohio 44115

Dear Ms. Lowery,

Judge Joseph Russo has assigned me to represent you in your Motion for Judicial Release. He has shared with me your letters, and accordingly, I am familiar with the circumstances which led to your plea as well as your experiences since that time.

In order to better represent you, I would like very much to meet with you. Please list me as your attorney at the Pre-Release Center and send me whatever paperwork I need to complete. I am enclosing two address labels for your convenience. Also, feel free to call my office at the telephone number listed above. I will accept your collect call. The best time to reach me is in the late afternoon and early evening.

Sincerely,

Elizabeth Kelley

P.S. Please note that my suite number is "1020" and that my fax number is "502-0765." The other information is the same.

encl.

cc: Judge Joseph Russo

Chapter Seven

After Four Extra Years of Incarceration, The Way I Was Released

Ultimately, God got me out of prison. My situation is proof that God answers prayer. The Hon. Judge Joseph Russo and Attorney Elizabeth Kelley were the instrumental people whose expertise and efforts resulted in my freedom from prison. However, as for items, I attribute my release from prison mainly to three aspects – an article about me that appeared in *The Free Times* publication, the Layne Law, and my domestic violence assessment.

But before I encountered those three components, during my incarceration, I tried to find a legal release from prison by writing many letters all over the world asking for help. People would write back to me providing me with some information but basically sent to me information directing me to someone else to which to write. As a result of my extensive writing activity, I acquired the nickname, "International". My very good friend, Carmen, who is a good writer, while incarcerated also wrote many letters worldwide.

Inmates were allowed one free envelope per week. They could send more letters if they wanted to, but they had to purchase the necessities for such at the commissary. An inmate could purchase a maximum of fifteen envelopes per week. Sometimes inmates traded with each other envelopes for other items.

I spent a lot of time in the prison's law library. My lawyer dismissed me. He had told me to plead guilty to my co-defendant's crime of murder, and I thought, "Why should I plead guilty to something I didn't do? I wasn't even present when the murder occurred." After my co-defendant did kill his victim, I did drive the car away. The lawyer told me that when someone is associated with a crime, the person who actually committed the crime and anyone associated with the criminal act is charged with the crime. Association was my situation and the situation of many of the other female inmates. At the time I was taken into custody, I was nervous, scared, and inexperienced in criminal affairs. Thus, at my lawyer's advice, I plea bargained complicity and had no jury trial. I went before a judge and prosecutor and got a twenty-two-year-to-life sentence with a possible death sentence by electrocution. If I would have been electrocuted, I would have been the first woman in Ohio to actually receive the death penalty. Fortunately, that never happened. In hindsight, I probably would have received a shorter sentence if I had had a jury trial. Perhaps if I had gone before twelve jurors, the jurors would have seen the real me.

Over the many years of imprisonment, I spent much time in the prison's library poring over books, trying to find a legal way to freedom. It's easy to get into prison but hard to get out. In 1996 I went before the parole board and was denied. I was informed that it would be another five years before I could appear before the parole board again. The people on that board were trying to make me serve twenty-five years in prison because of my classification. Then I went to the parole board again in 2001 and was again denied parole. At that time I was told that my next parole board appearance could be in three more years. The first sentencing judge I contacted was Judge Ann Dyke who eventually moved on to serving as a judge to an appellate court. Then I wrote many letters including several to Judge Patricia Cleary from whom I never received a reply and then began writing to Judge Joseph Russo, telling him about incidents in my life. I wrote to him every week. One day I received a letter from criminal defense attorney, Ms. Elizabeth Kelley, a person very dear to me for her superb legal ability and vivacious personality. Judge Russo had requested that Ms. Kelley investigate my case. I was overjoyed and surprised by Ms. Kelley's first letter to me that I treasure. Now the "door" was open. Ms. Kelley asked me, "Marilyn, would it be all right with you if I sent a reporter to interview you?" I enthusiastically replied, "Sure." The result was an article about me that appeared in the *Free Times* which was distributed around the city. The reporter brought about five hundred copies of the article for other inmates to read. However, prison system decision-makers said that I was the only person who could have a copy. Thus, I circumvented the system by allowing other inmates to read my copy of the article and pass it on to other inmates because I wanted other people to know what had happened. Since a multitude of Clevelanders around the city and many other inmates had read the publication's article, one day a CO, a guard, informed me, "Marilyn, you have become a celebrity!" I was delighted that my circumstances had been revealed to many others. For Ms. Kelley's activities in my behalf, from then on, when she visited me at the prison concerning my legal affairs, she got the "royal treatment" from many other inmates. When Ms. Kelley would arrive at the prison, some of the other inmates would say, "Here's Marilyn's lawyer." They would get her a table and put it before her and get her a chair. All of the other inmates were in awe of Ms. Kelley for her forthrightness in "stepping right into the door," after I had served twenty-two years of incarceration, demanding that I legally be released from prison. I tremendously wish to thank Ms. Kelley and the Honorable Joseph Russo for their efforts in enabling me to become free from prison so that I could come home to be with my dearly-loved family, especially my parents because I had only one set of them.

I believe that one of the main reasons I was released from prison was because of the article about me in the *Free Times* publication. As stated, involved people such as Ms. Kelley and others were instrumental in my prison release, but

I think that the central feature was that article which is a huge example of that well-known saying, "The Power of the Press." The article exposed the violation of prison inmates' constitutional rights. The publicity generated from that article exerted overwhelming pressure on parole boards whose members were basing their decisions of denying or granting parole for prison inmates on the prison inmate's original sentence instead of the plea-bargained sentence. The result was the Layne Law which compels parole board members to use an inmate's plea-bargained prison sentence as the criterion when determining the denial or consent to release prison inmates. Consequently, MANY prison inmates' cases were reviewed, resulting in numerous prison inmates being justifiably released from prisons.

According to what is called the "Syllabus of the Court," parole officers who comprise The Ohio Adult Parole Authority (APA) use what is called a "parole guidelines chart" to determine the range of time that a prisoner should serve before being released. When considering inmates for parole, the APA relies on a combination of two factors: the seriousness of the inmate's crime and the criminal offender's risk of what is called recidivism, that is the risk that inmate has of relapsing into crime, in other words, an attempt of parole board members to predict the possibility that if released, what would be the chances of that inmate of committing another crime or crimes? I was assigned the most serious category which was 13 whereas I should have actually been assigned a lower number that was appropriate for my plea bargain.

Specifically, at the parole hearing of an inmate by the name of Layne, the APA assigned him an offense category score for kidnapping despite the fact that the offense of kidnapping, while charged in the original indictment, was subsequently dropped by the prosecutor in exchange for Layne's plea. Thus, the result in Layne's case against the Ohio Adult Parole Authority was that Layne's constitutional rights were being violated. I was an inmate who benefited from the Layne Decision.

Possibly the third main reason that effected my release from prison was due to me having been a victim of domestic violence. My attorney, Ms. Kelly, asked the Director of Counseling and Community Services at the Domestic Violence Center to interview and assess me to discover if I was legitimately a victim of domestic violence that affected my initial response in the robbery aspect my co-defendant's crime.

My response to the sudden and brutally violent death of my husband in 1976 that I witnessed was what professional sociologists call Post-Traumatic Stress Disorder, producing a persistent sense of impending danger and threat, nightmares, and depression. At that time, I was also a twenty-one-year-old widow with the responsibilities of singly raising two little children. The interviewer stated that at the time, 1980, I met who turned out to be my co-defendant, I may have been especially vulnerable and impressionable. At that time I remember being gullible, afraid, and naïve. When I first met this man, I thought that he was a charming, confident man with money and nice clothes. According to this expert in the domestic violence subject, one revealing indication of abusive relationships is that the emotional attachment intensifies quickly. Couples progress toward marriage or joint living arrangements more rapidly than non-abusive couples. This man and I began living together after only three months after our first meeting.

During this interview, I recounted my relationship with this man. Some of the events I remember were verbal, physical, sexual, and psychological abuse. For example, one time I remember that he severely beat me because I didn't make cornbread for him. At that time, I was ill and was trying to take care of my children, two little girls. I remember another time after an episode of physical violence, he raped me. Several times, now I think to intimidate me, he would

61

sometimes place a loaded gun on a table if I did not appear to be complying with his wishes. Also, from time to time he made verbal threats of killing me and/or my children if I were to try to end my relationship with him. In addition, he relentlessly strove to control my associations with other people by isolating me from my family members and friends whom he alleged were lesbians.

During those times he had me so intimidated that I did not bring his behavior to the attention of authorities.

In addition, he exercised a pattern of threats designed to coerce me to engage in unwanted behaviors, some legal and some illegal. For example, he forced me into prostitution for which he collected payment. During the two years that I had a relationship with this man, he had a criminal record and was simultaneously on parole. At that time, I had no criminal record.

This specialist on domestic violence who interviewed me for examination of my situation believes that his pattern of coercion of me to commit criminal acts is crucial, believing that when this man was robbing the present patrons of this after hours joint and he instructed me to collect the people's money, like many battered women do, I did what I had become accustomed to doing which was to follow his instructions out of fear of retaliation and my perceived lack of alternatives. According to this lady, another typical characteristic of victims of Battered Women Syndrome is that this violent partner and I believed that I was the one whose fault it was for what happened that night that those crimes happened. This expert who interviewed me stated that proof of her assessment here is that when he and I were legally confronted with the crimes of that night, he pled not guilty, and I entered a guilty plea.

In retrospect, in addition to being degraded regarding the illegal acts of prostitution, I am ashamed that at that time I was so psychologically and emotionally weak, gullible, and naïve.

This professional in domestic violence concluded that when I met the man who eventually became my co-defendant, I was in a compromised psychological state due to the trauma of me having witnessed my husband's brutal murder, and the results of being solely responsible for the raising of my children.

The Director of Counseling and Community Services at the Domestic Violence Center who interviewed me concluded from her interview with me that my answers and behavior were consistent with the experience and characteristics of women suffering from Battered Women's Syndrome, the series of common characteristics that appear in women who are abused physically and psychologically over an extended period of time. This director also determined that I was a victim of what is called "Learned Helplessness" which is another aspect of Battered Women's Syndrome in which the female sufferer often does not know why she is beaten on any particular occasion. The violence is perceived by the woman as random and aversive stimulation. Because of its randomness, she believes that she is incapable of doing anything to prevent the abuse and, as a result, feels helpless. Furthermore, because of my economic situation then, I did not see a way out of the situation.

Therefore, this domestic violence specialist resolved that my continuous fear of imminent harm from my then partner, later co-defendant, may explain why I committed, participated in, or assisted him in the commission of the crimes for which I was incarcerated.

Chapter Eight

Transition From Prison Back Into Mainstream Society

The parole board told me that I could be released from prison in around 1 ½ months while necessary paperwork could be completed. Between the time I learned of my release and the time when I was actually released, I was a little tense because some other inmates who were jealous of an inmate being released would try to do something to delay or prevent the inmate from being released. For example, sometimes an inmate would try to pick a fight with the inmate who was scheduled to be released from prison. Another tactic that a jealous inmate might employ is to leave contraband, something that was against prison rules such as a radio or television, in the inmate's room once that inmate would leave her room, to get that inmate into trouble with prison officials. While still in prison, when other inmates discovered that I was going home, some of them asked for my items that I had in prison, so I began giving things away except music tapes. I was "crazy" about my music. "Lifers" wouldn't create waves. I gave some of my belongings to them because I believed that some of them were never going home. Also, I felt that after twenty-two years of incarceration, I would probably need new or improved items and because I was going to be free, I could buy new items. I was hoping that I could anyway, but I knew that I did not have a job or a man or boyfriend at the time I was released from prison.

The night before I was released from prison, my eyes were closed, but I didn't sleep; my mind was racing – freedom, freedom – the thought of leaving those four confining walls after TWENTY-TWO YEARS! I couldn't wait for the next morning to arrive, for it to get light outside. Somewhere between 8:00 a.m. and 8:30 a.m., inmates were called out of their rooms. Everything for me was like baby steps. Was this true that I was finally getting out of prison? Was this real? I had mixed feelings. I was not sure if my three children would call me "Mommy" or "Mother." I was afraid, scared "to death," and nervous because of the unknowns of facing mainstream society again after such a long time – twenty-two years! I remember an inmate who was elderly when I had known her in 1982 when I had gone to prison. She had been a maid for a family and had poisoned one of the family members. I remember that she was a foreigner. She had been brought to prison in a horse and buggy. After many years of serving time in prison for what she had done, she was finally released from prison. When she was released, there were cars and other changes which were too much for her mentally. She "cracked up" because she just couldn't adjust to living in mainstream society again after such a long time of being absent from it. She was brought back to prison where she eventually passed away when she was eighty or eighty-plus years of age. The prison buried her deceased body. Just prior to my release, I had a good idea of how this lady must have felt. Some inmates get out of prison with intentions of doing well and staying on the right side of the law, but some people in society will not give to them a chance, so they become confused and don't know where to go and who to turn to, thus becoming depressed. As a result, some of them slip into or back into drug or alcohol abuse and resort to committing other crimes, stealing to support their drug habits. Therefore, some of them end up going back to prison. I knew I wanted to be a law abiding citizen, but other than that, I didn't know what I was going to do once I was out of prison. However, I WAS EXCITED! I was getting out!!!!!!!!!!!!!! During my incarceration, there were times when I thought I'd never get out of prison alive. I'd seen so many inmates pass away while I was in prison.

65

Some inmates exiting prison have nowhere to go, so they go to a halfway house where there are rules and regulations; it's like being in prison. However, in my case, I was blessed with a loving family who cared about me and who would let me live with them, which is what I told prison officials – that I'd stay with my family.

When being released from prison, prison officials gave to me $75.00 in cash. This money comes from the state. Upon exiting prison, each inmate is given the $75.00 plus any money that is in her account at that time. The inmate's account is closed one week before the inmate is released from prison. That's all the money I had at the time. When I was given the money, it looked so "funny." I hadn't touched money for twenty-two years. The money looked big and phony. I had a weird feeling, but I was happy nevertheless!

Then came my actual release from prison. As I exited the prison gates on that glorious day, there were some inmates on the inside of the fence yelling to me, "Bye" and "Marilyn, we love you. Take care." I was waving "Bye" to them. I had previously gotten contact information of some of the inmates who I had associated with in prison. On this day, some of the inmates drew cards to give to me. I had mixed feelings – sadness of leaving some of the other inmates but had an overwhelming feeling of joy, a wonderful feeling of seeing and being around some of my family members and friends outside of prison again. I was so happy to be able to get back to my children and parents and to spend time with them. On the other side of the gate, my three unspeakably dear children and exceedingly wonderful grandchildren were waiting for me along with other family members. There was a slew of people there to greet me on the outside of those prison gates. They had various colors of balloons which they let ascend into the air. My greeters hugged and kissed me. I was so very happy to be in the company of my precious family again and to get out of that place! It was a great feeling! I remember one inmate telling me that when she was released from prison, she literally kissed the ground, and I wanted to kiss it also.

After some photographs were taken, we got into cars and left. During the drive home, things looked strange to me. Some places had been torn down. The cars along the way were models that I had not seen before and were therefore new to me. I saw people using cell phones. I felt like I had come from a different country. Now I know how foreigners feel when they come to the United States. But all I knew was that I had freedom again (except for being on parole for five years) in my life.

I visited my two parents that day and then was taken to my eldest daughter's hair salon where my daughter did my hair. My children had bought me clothes, shoes, jewelry and personal things. I got all prettied up for the big welcome home party that my dear children had planned for me the evening of that memorable day.

The party that evening was fantastic. It was so wonderful to be around my family members and friends again, and people brought me presents. Although I was very happy, it all seemed so weird. I guess at that time I had become unaccustomed to such surroundings and activities having been in prison for such a long time.

I was thinner when I left prison because I had routinely worked out, especially after I had had my last child. I didn't want to look like I had just given birth.

Upon reflection, I would NEVER want to return to prison. I never want to go through that again. It was terrible! Prison is a very lonely place even if an inmate has friends to talk with. There is no family around. Occasionally I could talk with people over a telephone for twenty or thirty minutes. If the person on the other end of the line told me that I sounded depressed, the person would tell me to call again, but I knew that that would entail another bill. The telephone bills in Marysville were very high but much less expensive in the Pre-Release Center.

I was released from prison on a Friday and then the party that evening. On the following Monday, I had to see a parole officer who gave to me a urine test probably to see if I had taken any illegal drugs over the weekend. I passed the test. Also, at this visit to my then parole officer, I was given the rules and regulations for being on parole.

My Release With My Family

My Mother, Me, And Mother-In-Law On My Release Day

NORTHEAST PRE-RELEASE CENTER

CERTIFICATE OF RECOGNITION

PRESENTED TO

MARILYN LOWERY

WITH GRATEFUL APPRECIATION FOR MAKING STRIDES
AGAINST BREAST CANCER WALK-A-THON

This 20th day of MAY, 2006

Co-Chair   Co-Chair

Chapter Nine

The Injustice of the Incarceration System and Unfair Sentencing

I think that there are some injustices in the United States' justice system. A judge does not seem to take into account the inmate's circumstances because judges seem to just want to charge the offender with a crime or by just using whatever they see written in black and white. I think that a fairer way for judges to sentence convicted people would be for judges to use a broader approach by considering the people's circumstances. I never had a police record, but my co-defendant did, so I felt that I was penalized because of him. The court does not want to hear anything about *why* a person committed a crime. It seems to me that members of the judicial system have a book with one set of rules that states that a person is guilty regardless. It seemed to me that African American convicted criminals received more prison time than Caucasian Americans for the same types of crimes. Thus, I think that the judicial system is prejudiced, or at least was back when I was experiencing this phase of the process. Sometimes I feel that some judges want people to be locked up forever, until the inmates pass away from this world. Most inmates in prison have psychological problems, but judges do not consider those problems. Prison, to me, is a multi-million dollar business, and the more inmates there are, the more money various people make. Some people's enormous material wealth is a result of the incarceration of mostly downtrodden people, some people who are imprisoned for their natural lives; some people's great wealth is at the expense of less fortunate, poor and/or poverty-stricken people. This situation is also at the expense of anyone who is employed and pays taxes because part of taxpayers' money is used to house and take care of prison inmates. Now that I am home I often think about judges and prosecutors and ask myself rhetorically why they are so mean. The people they sentence are human beings like they are. Honestly, I believe that God is the real Judge of everyone's life, and just like the rest of us, these officials will all have to eventually face God's judgment including their actions as judges. I think that there are good judges and bad judges. Each of us has only one life in this world.

I might add that perhaps the prison term-parole situation needs to be further examined and possibly adjusted or changed. For example, I served a twenty-two-year prison sentence, and after I was released, I was on parole for another five years. Parole is, in some ways, similar to being in prison. Even though being on parole allows a former prison inmate *more* freedoms than prison inmates have, parole has some restrictions also; a parolee is not truly, completely free, so viewing the situation from this perspective, I served a restricted sentence of twenty-seven years (twenty-two years in prison and another five years of parole.)

After a person commits a crime and is thus considered a menace to society, a threat to other people's safety, that person is temporarily or permanently removed from mainstream society by being incarcerated. However, in addition to that, if the US justice system is *truly* interested in these criminals becoming useful or at least harmless members of society, the US justice system is structured in such a way as to send to jail many people who do not have to be there. Whether I am accurate or inaccurate, my opinion is that more people are put into prisons than have to be there because every year prisons get so much money per inmate. Instead, these people could be sent to treatment centers where the professional personnel at these centers could better address the problems and rehabilitation of these wayward people. In the interest of *sincere* rehabilitation of incarcerated people, I do not think that such a large portion of inmates need to be medicated to the extent that many of them are. Some inmates become "walking pill bottles." Instead of prison decision-makers causing inmates to be what I consider unnecessary overuse of pills for inmates, more rehabilitative success could be accomplished to reform inmates by producing more group meetings. For example, it was at group meetings that I discovered that I had been in an abusive relationship. I think that there should be more group gatherings to teach male and female victims of domestic abuse, for instance, how to cope with that issue.

The workings of prisons include the distribution of various items such as undergarments. Some inmates have no money; they don't have families, or their families don't care about them, so these inmates have to rely on what and when items are given to them, which sometimes involve long periods of time. People outside of prison may think that all inmates get what they deserve, but even inmates are human beings.

Believe it or not, it costs money to live in prison. Also, it goes without saying that an inmate fares much better if he or she has someone on the outside taking care of the inmate's business affairs, but some inmates don't have anyone.

I think that another improvement that could be made in the prison system is that guards need to be better scrutinized. Some women inmates have babies from some male guards. Some male guards are needed in women's prisons because some female inmates can occasionally become very unruly which sometimes requires the physical strength of men such as breaking up fights of female inmates.

Another improvement in the prison system would be to serve inmates more nutritional food. There seems to be an excessive or possibly an unhealthy amount of starch in food given to prisoners. I think that better dietitians should oversee the prison food. Furthermore with regards to food, I think that inmates are not given adequate amounts of food; they are like children's portions, and are given too early for the final meal of each day. Most inmates are hungry later in the evening during waking hours. I'm not saying that inmates should be treated royally, just humanely.

Moreover, I think that there should be better doctors, certified doctors, to treat inmates. There are many medical mistakes made; many times inmates are given wrong medications, and there seems to be more misdiagnoses for inmates than in the public sector. I saw many people die in prison – some from negligence and some because it was their time, I guess.

I also think that another improvement would be to start college opportunities for inmates like before. Many people in society who are outside of prisons may argue that a portion of their tax money is already being used to house inmates, so why should these people in society who are outside of prisons also pay for inmates' college educations? Upon examining the situation and temporarily putting aside the politics of this issue, the US government is already providing college educations for various Americans through grants and in other ways. Some people may be against that policy, but that is a present reality. If people who create and maintain the US justice system are *genuinely* interested in rehabilitating errant people whose decisions and actions in their lives have landed them in prison, inmates should be given the opportunity to further their education at the college level. Striving to obtain a college education for an inmate instead of the inmate just sitting around day by day hoping that he or she will eventually get out of prison, gives the inmate something constructive to do and moves that inmate towards becoming a constructive citizen.

Prison is a nightmare. People might rightly say that making prison an unattractive place in which to be may be a deterrent for some people who might otherwise commit crimes, but I think that the changes I have discussed here would improve society as a whole.

Chapter Ten

Life After Prison

Consequences of Having Been In Prison

After I was released from prison, I was on parole for five years. I was released from prison in the custody of my eldest daughter. She was like my guardian which was a role reversal that caused friction. She acted like she was my mother, and that angered me, so I didn't live with her for long. I moved in with my parents who then became my guardians. I helped to take care of them. My parents' house was a grand place. It was made of good quality beautiful-looking wood and an appealing fireplace. This huge house included five bedrooms. When I moved into their house after my prison term, my parents were older and didn't have the money to keep the house in good condition, so their house had fallen somewhat into disrepair. If I would have had the money, I would have had their majestic house fixed up.

I had to tell a parole officer of my move from my eldest daughter's house to my parents' house. I wasn't sure if my parole officer would let me live in my parents' house because of the house's dilapidated condition then, but I was allowed to reside in their house. Eventually I moved to my own place. One of the problems a former prison inmate can encounter is difficulty when finding a place in which to live independently. When potential landlords discover via applications or otherwise that the possible tenant has been in prison, many landlords are leery to rent to the former prison inmate. Nevertheless, when I was able to rent a place, from then on I was responsible only to the parole officer.

I wanted a car. During my long time of incarceration,

I had lost touch with mainstream society. For example, when I first got onto a bus, I didn't know where to put the money. After twenty-two years the people and bus looked so weird to me. Also, I was released from prison close to the beginning of winter in 2003. I would get cold waiting for buses, so sometimes I'd hitchhike. My daughters advised me not to hitchhike telling me that things aren't like they used to be when a person could trust most other people, but I never had any problems. My eldest daughter told me that I should get a driver's license. I had not driven for twenty-two years, and my driver's license had expired. I had been locked up for so long that I actually forgot how to drive. Thus, I had to take a written driver's test and an actual driving test again in order to obtain my new driver's license. I failed the driver's test the first two times but passed it the third time.

I was still getting updated with changes. I was so outdated with everything. For examples, I had to learn how to use a cell phone and a television remote which my granddaughter showed me how to use since in prison we manipulated the television by buttons on the television. There were no remotes in prison. Everyone in prison could buy a television or have one sent into the prison from family members; however, now an inmate has to order a television.

After being released from prison, I also had to find a good doctor to take care of me medically, and re-registering to vote was another task I did after being out of mainstream society for so long.

Monetarily, after seven years, a person's outstanding debts are "wiped clean". However, another potential consequence, one that a newly released prison inmate must guard against, is falling prey to the flood of credit card pre-approvals that are sent to the former inmate. In my case, before my prison years, I had been married, and my husband had really done the working. I had a few jobs occasionally but had not had much experience in the working world. Then for the twenty-two years that I was in prison, my parents, sister, and my children when they got older, sent to me items that I would have normally shopped for myself if I had not been incarcerated at the time. I am grateful to my wonderful family members who were so kind to me to send these items to me and that, in my opinion, had good taste in clothing, shoes and such. Then, after I was newly released from prison, I was sent MANY unsolicited credit cards that already had my name on them. People from these credit card companies sent me these cards, and at the time, I had no job. I couldn't believe it! I ended up having twenty-one credit cards – yes, twenty-one! Having not shopped for twenty-two years and then suddenly having the means to do all of the shopping I wanted to, and at the time of purchase, not required to produce cash money on the spot since I could buy items using credit cards, I went on wild shopping sprees over a period of time. After living in prison in a rather unadorned way for so long and then at stores seeing so many pretty clothes, shoes and perfumes, I went totally wild with shopping, even though I had no employment so had no paychecks. Having credit cards is like having candy in a bank. Shopping was so much fun until the bills started piling up! When I was relentlessly inundated with bills and harassing calls from credit card collectors, I did not know what direction to pursue or who to talk with about the problem I found myself in. Eventually I was able to consolidate my credit card bills with a company that manages credit card purchases. Consequently, the day and night harrying telephone calls stopped. Through this company I am slowly paying off these credit card bills. Concerning credit cards, I wish I could have "turned back the hands of time" immediately after being released from prison so that I could have possibly avoided this credit card bind. If I have a credit card in the future, I will use it discretionarily. Common sense will prevail. These credit card companies have become so wealthy because when a person does not pay the full balance owed for each bill, there is a fee attached to the cost of the item(s) purchased on credit. I think that credit card companies constitute a moneymaking machine also. I urge anyone exiting prison to be conscious of the fact that he or she is an easy victim for people who are behind issuing credit cards. A newly-released prison inmate is potentially vulnerable to credit card issuers. Thus, beware of accepting and using many credit cards because that credit card user could be in debt for the rest of her or his life as a result. That, in turn, will give that person a bad credit rating which may hurt the person if that person tries to apply for a loan such as for a house or other big purchase.

I received help from many other people. I thought that now that my children are grown, they could buy me items if I needed them since I had no job. An organization called Community Re-entry which assisted people who have been in prison helped me very much. They gave me food if I wanted it and clothes. In addition, some churches helped me. One church even gave to me several pieces of furniture. I was well-known from the *Free Times* article about me.

During the five years that I was on parole after being in prison, I had three parole officers to whom I had to report. I was required to pay the parole officer at the time $20.00 a month. These parole officers were all "cool." Sometimes I went to Pennsylvania. Whenever I went out of state, beforehand I had to report to my parole officer to obtain a paper. During my journeys, if I would have been stopped by a police officer and did not have that paper, I would have been in violation of my parole. After the completion of those five years, I was truly free again, at least from having to be monitored.

Family

Regarding some of my family members, I think that my youngest daughter is very different than my older two daughters. I'm not saying that in any kind of judgmental way by any means; I'm just saying, different. I think that another possible outcome of me having been imprisoned for so long of a time is that my youngest daughter seems to me to be a little more distant with me than my other two children. I guess it would stand to reason because my youngest daughter was raised daily by my mother and not by me since I was incarcerated at the time, for the first twenty-two years of my youngest daughter's life. As she said when interviewed one of the times I was on a local news television broadcast, that she has two mothers. I think that my parents spoiled my youngest daughter much as she was growing up. I presently feel guilty that I cannot help my children financially. I think that they should be able to come to me and say that they need occasional monetary assistance if/when they do.

In addition to currently feeling guilty about my present financial inability to assist my children when needed, when I was no longer in prison, I felt a little guilty that I had been unable to help my parents, at least healthwise, because of my imprisonment. My siblings said that they had helped my parents in various aspects when I was away, incarcerated, of which I am appreciative. I hope that at least in the health arena, during the years of my incarceration, my parents probably didn't need a lot of help.

My precious father lived for three years after my prison release. He passed away from heart complications, passing away in my arms on a Christmas Day 2004. While I was in prison, he had a pacemaker put in, and he possibly didn't get new batteries in it or something. After I got out of prison, my father and I did not get along well. I think that my father was somewhat angry with me. I think his anger stemmed from him possibly thinking that his daughter had gotten into trouble, having done something badly enough to cause her to serve such a long prison sentence. After my incarceration, I think that my father considered me a family outcast. He treated me differently after I had come home from prison. When I lived with my parents after serving my prison term, sometimes my father and I argued a lot. I tried not to say or do anything that would cause him to argue with me. Although there was frequent disharmony between my father and me after my incarceration, I know that my father always loved me, and I loved him. During the time that I lived with my parents post-prison, my father got dementia. Sadly, just prior to his earthy demise, he must have sensed that his life in this world was drawing to an end because I remember the day before Christmas of the year he passed away, my father told one of my nephews, "This will be the last time I will be cutting up turkey for Christmas Day." During this time in my parents' lives, they could no longer climb stairs, so they converted a room on the main floor to a bedroom. On that Christmas morning, I got up and told my parents that I would cook breakfast which I did. My father said that he did not want to eat anything, so my mother and I ate breakfast together. Then I went upstairs. One of my nephews called me downstairs, saying that something was wrong with my father. Upon entering the room, I saw my father lying in bed of which he had gotten out of briefly to use the washroom the day he passed away, and when I looked at him, he seemed like he was choking, but I knew that he had had not eaten anything. I immediately told my brother to call 911 emergency. The person on the other end of the telephone line asked me, "What is he doing now?" I responded, "Choking." Paramedics came and tried to work with my father in the bedroom. Meanwhile, my precious mother was nervously sitting in the dining room repeatedly saying, "He's not going to make it." The paramedics took my father out of the house and into an ambulance which stayed in the front of the house for I'd say around twenty to thirty minutes and then pulled away with no siren sounding and no lights flashing. My brother went to the hospital and came back around a half hour later. My brother came upstairs. I asked him what the situation was with our father. My brother *calmly* replied, "Daddy died." I was just devastated, but I was so grateful that I had been able to spend some time with him after I had gotten out of prison.

My father's name was spelled "Carol" but pronounced "Carl." The name of one of my brothers is "Carl," but he is called "Chuck." My father had never graduated from high school and had served in the army. I admired my father. My father and mother had ten children together, and he stayed with my mother and worked hard during his life in this world.

My dear mother lived in this world for eight years after my prison release. She had two houses – the house in which she and my father lived and the house that she inherited from her mother. Sadly though, my mother lost both houses due to foreclosure. When my father was still living in this world, being a veteran of the United States armed forces, and my parents were faced with foreclosure, my father sought assistance from the VA but received no help. I thought that my mother losing the house in which my parents had lived was such a sad situation because my father had worked his whole working life for that house, and then that house was taken afterwards. By the time that my mother had to move from her house to an apartment, living by herself, I had my own place in which to live. I stored some of my mother's belongings. I visited my mother often when she lived in her apartment, and my youngest daughter also helped very much. I speculate that my youngest daughter possibly had a unique bond with my mother because my parents had raised her pretty much from the time that this daughter of mine was an infant to the age of twenty-two years while I was incarcerated.

My mother did not drink alcoholic beverages, in fact really had no vices, but my precious, poor mother physically suffered much near to the end of her life in this world. She had high blood pressure and diabetes to the extent that her toes had to be amputated. I think that her health condition which culminated in her physical death in this world started when she complained that her neck hurt, the cause which was later discovered to be cancer. She eventually developed breast cancer. I suppose that there could have been various reasons why the cancer developed. My mother did not smoke, but I would guess that one possibility could be that she may have inhaled secondhand smoke for years from other family members who did smoke. Doctors who were treating my mother said that operation was unwise because of her other health problems, so the doctors gave my mother medicines to treat the cancer. However, her breast cancer eventually spread to her spine and lungs, ultimately killing her. Near to the end of my mother's life in this world, doctors suggested Hospice for her. I called a meeting of my family members to address my mother's situation. My eldest daughter and one of my sisters stayed where my mother was when my mother passed away. I remember that I was home cleaning when I received a call from a family member to tell me that my mother had passed away. The day was March 5, 2011, fifteen days shy of my mother's eighty-first birthday. My eldest daughter who owns a well-known hair salon lovingly and expertly prepared my deceased mother's hair, nails, jewelry and make up.

When I had gotten out of prison, having been legally released from prison, during my mother's medical problems throughout the last few years of her life in this world, I exerted a colossal effort to assist and care for my mother. I very much attended her during her final years in this world. Sometimes an older person becomes like a child in some ways, dependent in some ways. I think that a common problem in the USA today is that many younger people don't want to be bothered taking care of older loved ones, people who brought them into the world and loved and helped them no matter what they may have done, as was in my case. My mother was a wonderful woman who loved me very much and was always generous with me. I loved my mother very much, and I miss her, but I take comfort in knowing that my mother is in a better and safe place now and is with my father. I realize that that is the way life works; we are born to die. In retrospect, my mother lived a happy and long life. Also, I'm glad that my mother met the man I am presently with and that my mother and my man liked each other.

After my mother had passed away, we family members went through my mother's belongings, and people took what they wanted. I have some of my mother's costume jewelry and had my mother's effects in a storage bin. Sometimes I go through her possessions and either throw some items away or give some of them to other people. I would like to move from my present location, and before doing so, I would like to have my mother's personal property gone as I have enough of my own effects. One discomforting situation I presently have is the size of the house in which I reside. I would like to live in a larger house, preferably a house that I would own instead of renting. That way I would have more freedom to do things to the house that I do not have the authority to do in a rented house that is owned by someone else. My present house is too small to enable me to keep my possessions organized. When I was caring for my ailing mother during the last few years that she spent in this world, I would have much preferred to have had her live with me in the same house instead of her living in a nursing home, but I did not have the room and necessary accommodations for her. The house in which I lived had an inadequate amount of necessary space in which another person could live. The reality was that my house was just too small. Also, the house was not suited to her needs. For example, the width of the doorways in my house are too small for her motorized chair to fit through. I would like some help with getting my own home. All of the houses I have lived in have been small. There seems to be no room. One day I will get a HUGE house.

My mother had visions like I had. For example, when my husband was shot and killed, my mother sensed that something had happened. She always felt, sensed, when something was wrong. It was just a feeling she got.

For some reason, my mother believed that people who have hazel eyes are no good. Coincidently or appropriately, my co-defendant has hazel eyes. My mother told me to get away from him. She said to me concerning my co-defendant, "Ree (most people call me that because my middle name is Marie), "you need to leave him alone and go about your business." I guess her belief has affected my thinking on the matter; I will never go with a man who has hazel eyes. I've learned my lesson. My co-defendant, his mother, and his sister have hazel eyes. When my youngest daughter was born, my co-defendant being her father, I couldn't wait until she opened her eyes so that I could make sure that she does not have hazel eyes. She doesn't.

At the time of this writing, I guess like most families, some of my other family members have medical issues, but at least now, to the best of my knowledge, none of them have cancer.

My Loving Parents

Some Of My Family Members

Romantic Relationships/Friendships

Being a woman, I have had and have special relationships with several men throughout my life so far. In addition to the significant men in my life so far of whom I have previously expounded, there was Gary, a bus driver, with whom I lived prior to my prison days and who has passed away since I have been out of prison. Then there was Frederick who I met in my post-prison years. I met Frederick at a racetrack. He was an elderly man many years my senior who I thought was dressed rather seedily when I met him. He told me to come to his house, so I did. Based on his shabby appearance, I expected him to live in a fairly crummy house, but I was quite mistaken. He dwelled in an exceedingly beautiful house on attractive sprawling grounds. His house included a very attractive, stately fireplace constructed of stones, and the grounds contained a picturesque, hand-dug lake with an extended, wooden walkway that jutted out across part of the pond. At that time I sometimes collected scrap metal and turned it in for money. Frederick wanted me to take the scrap metal he had around his yard which would clean up his yard. I don't see anything wrong with a person carrying on a romantic-type relationship with someone from another group, racial or ethnic. Frederick was Hungarian, ethnic to the extent that he spoke English with an accent. Frederick was a nice man who was good to me. For example, he gave to me two cars, but eventually he hurt me because in time he dismissed me because I was a member of a group that is different than his faction. And I was not used to being dismissed. I am usually the one who does the dismissing of amorous relationships. However, for quite a while now, I have been involved in a very special relationship with my present soul mate.

Furthermore, I have a valued, platonic friendship with a diversely capable person, a man who used to live on the same street that I do. When I was taking care of my mother, I met a man named Keith Charles Ruff at the recreation center on Fulton Road. At that time he was seventy-nine years old, and I have always had a strong affinity for taking care of elderly people. He told me that he was living with his stepson but because his stepson brought his son and his son's wife to live with him, Mr. Ruff had to move. He went to live with his stepson's daughter. For a while, this living arrangement worked satisfactorily, but Mr. Ruff eventually moved out of the stepson's daughter's house because he did not think that he was being treated well. Mr. Ruff is visually impaired, having had use of only one of his eyes. He had cataracts and glaucoma but was able to function well enough then to live alone. Then he had an eye operation, but before that medical procedure, the doctor said that after the operation, Mr. Ruff would have a 50% chance of seeing with his eyes. Unfortunately, after the eye operation, Mr. Ruff lost the little sight that he had had. Now he can just see shadows sometimes. Since I have been caring for Mr. Ruff, one day he was having trouble with one of his legs, so I called the emergency squad to take him to a hospital. After his diagnosis, he was temporarily sent to a rehabilitation center where he stayed for three weeks. In the meantime, I talked with his landlord who told me that he did not want Mr. Ruff to return to his house. I do know that Mr. Ruff had paid his rent on time. I do not understand why this landlord would not allow Mr. Ruff to return to his house, but since this landlord put this eighty-three-year-old man out of his house, I paid some men to help me move Mr. Ruff's belongings into my house. At the time of this writing, Mr. Ruff lives in the house with my man and me. He is too old now to live by himself, and I do not think he should live alone anyway due to his present vision situation. When Mr. Ruff and I became friends, I think that caused some jealousy in his stepdaughter, so she did not like him to be around me because she did not like me. Mr. Ruff has one daughter who does not live in Cleveland, Ohio, where I am living now, but lives in another state. However, I think that she does not want to be bothered with him. In reminiscence of the size of my house with regards to my mother being unable to live with me, in my taking care of Mr. Ruff, it is more convenient to have him live in the same house that my man and I do. However, as Mr. Ruff is now in a wheelchair all of the time, the lower level of the house which I am renting is really too small, and even before Mr. Ruff lived in the same house as I do, my rented house is too small, causing me to feel like I am still in prison, but I cannot afford a larger space. I would really like to live in a significantly larger house that would adequately accommodate three people, and own that house. I put my story on gofundle.com, but so far no one has offered to help me with my problem. I know that someday all of us who live long in this world will get old, and if I do, I would want someone to take care of me if needed because I do not want to be in a nursing home, and Mr. Ruff does not want to either.

Educational Attainments

While in prison, I thought that if a person wants to get anywhere in life, the person needs at least a GED, the equivalency of a high school diploma, and I thought that being in prison, I had the time, and I wanted to better myself. I took the GED seven times until I finally passed it. Many times determination is the difference between success and failure, and I was determined to obtain this educational achievement. Also, while serving my prison sentence, I completed the program to be a cosmetology instructor, manager, and obtained my appropriate operator license in 1996. After I was released from prison, I attended a local community college, Cuyahoga Community College, and earned an Associate of Arts in Liberal Arts degree in May of 2007. After obtaining that two-year degree, I moved on to Cleveland State University where I earned a Bachelor of Arts degree in Criminology in December 2010. After obtaining my four-year college degree, I felt a sense of self-gratification in my educational achievements after having been a young adult who had been exceedingly deficient in reading and writing. It helps to really want something. Since October 2012, I have been enrolled in Strayer University actively pursuing a Master's degree.

Cleveland State University

College of Liberal Arts and Social Sciences

THE PRESIDENT AND THE BOARD OF TRUSTEES OF CLEVELAND STATE UNIVERSITY

UPON RECOMMENDATION OF THE FACULTY HAVE CONFERRED UPON

Marilyn Marie Lowery

THE DEGREE OF

Bachelor of Arts

IN RECOGNITION OF THE SATISFACTORY FULFILLMENT OF THE REQUIREMENTS

PERTAINING TO THIS DEGREE CONFERRED AT CLEVELAND, OHIO,

THIS EIGHTEENTH DAY OF DECEMBER, TWO THOUSAND TEN.

CHAIRMAN OF THE BOARD OF TRUSTEES

PRESIDENT OF THE UNIVERSITY

DEAN

Struck By Cancer and Have Overcome

After I was released from prison, one day I noticed a small lump under my skin in one of my breasts. That lump seemed like part of a peanut. I then saw a doctor about it. Upon examining the lump, the doctor ordered an x-ray be taken of it. That doctor saw something suspicious and therefore sent me to another hospital to have other tests taken. A doctor at the second medical facility saw an abnormal spot so decided that this spot be removed. After the removed tissue was examined in a medical lab, the lump was shown to be cancerous. I was devastated! I thought, "After I had struggled to get through those long, horrible twenty-two years of prison and had survived that, I now had cancer, another imprisonment." When I had cancer, I thought that maybe by me smoking, that this habit might cause me to lose my life. When a doctor tells you that you have cancer, many fearful thoughts ripple through your mind. At least that is how I reacted. The most obvious one was "Will I live or is this the end of my life in this world? Should I kill myself? If I die tomorrow, what about my children?" There were other thoughts that also greatly disturbed me. "If I do survive, will I have to undergo a removal of one of my breasts? If that were to occur, would men still consider me desirable? Would my sex life be over or become markedly diminished? Would men still love me?" However, based on the medical evidence of my then situation, surgeons removed the lump and my lymph nodes that were in my armpit, but not my breast. From what I understand, though, that women who do have to have their breasts removed, modern technology can very much come to the rescue which results in a very minimal difference so that affected women's lives can continue very much the same as before they became afflicted with cancer. In my case, after my medical procedure had been concluded, I was given thirty-five radiation treatments. I hated that treatment because I had to be at the hospital everyday to receive this treatment. I had to lie down on a table, and a light was shown under my arm. I reached a point in time during this treatment that I almost gave up because I was tired of doing this activity every day. Granted though, this treatment was literally life saving. Also, given the circumstances of me having cancer, there were two characteristics for which I was fortunate and am grateful: according to the medical people involved in my condition, I did not require chemotherapy which has the side effect of the patient's hair falling out, and I did not have cancer while I was in prison. In my opinion, the medical people who service prison inmates for medical ailments are incompetent. By the time I developed cancer, at least I was out of prison and could therefore be treated by doctors whom I thought were more bona fide. Now, as far as I know, I no longer have cancer. Notwithstanding, the cancer medicine I had to take for awhile eventually caused another problem which led to me undergoing a total hysterectomy. Although I have no cancer now, as far as I know, I still sometimes wonder what will happen. I feel like I do not have cancer, but does cancer ever really go away? After all, my mother did pass away from lung cancer.

Although I am not a medical expert, it appears to me that cancer can "run" in families, that there is sometimes a heredity factor involved. At the time, it seemed as if my mother's cancer first appeared in one of her breasts. However, because of her other medical ailments such as having high blood pressure, diabetes to the extent that her toes had to be amputated, needing the use of a colostomy bag, a kidney problem that required regular dialysis, her doctors decided that she was too fragile to be operated on for her cancer, so the doctors decided to treat my mother's cancer problem using another approach which was by prescribing medicine. Eventually though, the cancer spread to her lungs which was the cause of my mother's passing away from this world.

After my release from prison, I discovered that my eldest daughter has also had cancer, specifically in her leg, a large tumor.

My mother and daughter who have had cancer never smoked. I do. I guess that smoking is a bad habit, but smoking is easy to get hooked on doing. Although I am not a medical person, I have heard that smoking directly or regularly inhaling second-hand smoke can greatly increase a person's chance of acquiring cancer, and when I had cancer, I thought that maybe by me smoking, that this habit might cause me to lose my life.

I empathize with people who would tell me that they had some kind of medical problem because I know how that is, but I guess that everyone has to eventually pass away from this world sooner or later. However, I am a strong person, and I will not let this problem get me down. My life will be my life. I do want to emphasize to people that it is very important for women to examine their breasts. If I had not done that, I would not have found that spot that I had. It is also very important for men to also check themselves or be checked for signs of possible prostate gland cancer. I was fortunate that my radiation came out well. I guess that I need to stop smoking and eat better foods since I think that eating health food is a significant factor in preventing a person from getting cancer. However, quitting smoking and learning to continuously eat healthy foods are easier said than done. When I was involved with the cancer walk-a-thon, I never dreamed that I would ever have cancer. I guess that my endeavor and then developing cancer was a coincidence.

It is very important for women to examine their breasts and for men to also check themselves or be checked for prostate gland cancer to look for signs of cancer.

Written and Broadcast Media Exposure

Possibly my troublesome dilemmas can be used to cause other people to avert such miserable situations. In addition to the immense and proven-to-be exceedingly important article about me in the *Free Times* publication which did facilitate the release of many incarcerated individuals, including me, who were having their constitutional rights violated, a chapter about me with an accompanying photograph of me is included in the book, *Inner Lives.* Then since my years of incarceration, different segments about me have appeared twice on a televised news station, May 2006 and May 2007, and I was a guest on an episode of the talk show, *West Views,* in March 2010. I have also spoken to various groups in attempts to encourage people to strive to lead prudent lives to hopefully avoid dreadful experiences like mine. In the future, I hope to provide more such talks to various audiences.

Dear Marilyn!

Thanks so much for sharing your story (again) with Channel 3 News! I'm so proud of you! Just think of all the people you've inspired, and all the "good" you're about to do!!

:)

Thanks again,

Kristin

My Endeavors

Employment

As a caregiver, I presently am closely attentive to an elderly gentleman, Mr. Ruff, who really has no one else in this world. I must say, though, that having fallen into unwise pursuits that landed me in prison, one is never entirely free again, at least in this world. Prison has its own restraints, parole other restrictions although fewer than prison life, but then when trying so seek legitimate employment, that criminal record continues to haunt you; potential employers would rather not hire people with formal, criminal records. It's rough.

Many times determination is the difference between success and failure.

Chapter Eleven

Information Learned and My Thoughts

As for domestic violence, I had been raised in a two-parent household with five brothers and four sisters. Throughout the years of growing up in my family, I witnessed no domestic violence, nor did I during the years of my own wholesome family composed of my dear-departed husband and two older daughters.

Five years later, my experience with domestic violence started months after I had been keeping company with the man who eventually became my co-defendant. My co-defendant started off as being nice as most men do, but then after a few months he became brutal with me. In my opinion love is not supposed to hurt but domestic violence sure does. Is savagery against one's romantic mate love or what? Domestic violence can produce severe results such as the victim losing an eye, a fractured jaw, getting her teeth knocked out, just to mention a few of the dreadful consequences, and even death. Since women are generally the physically weaker gender, they are usually the sorry victims of domestic violence of a physical nature.

In present times women can visit a website to discover if the man she is interested in has a criminal record but many times cannot tell if he is abusive until he actually displays harmful behavior. For us women who are naturally attracted to men, I guess that is a chance we women take when we initially begin special relationships with men. A problem is that how does a person just discard her feelings for another person? Maybe a person cannot "have her cake and eat it too!" Perhaps that is something to think about. In the past when I was with my co-defendant, I was unfamiliar with domestic violence, was more innocent to it, and being younger at that time, I was generally less experienced in life and therefore weaker which allowed me to be an easier target of domestic violence. In my case, in addition to suffering the immediate physical and psychological maltreatment, my abuse had far-reaching consequences. It led me to me being incarcerated for twenty-two years plus not being completely free for the five years that I was on post-prison parole. Domestic violence led me to spend the bulk of my younger and middle-aged years of my life behind bars. Furthermore, all of my dreams were shattered when this nightmare happened. It has taken me twenty-five years to tell my abuse story. I held it inside for years along with missing my family and being incarcerated for years. If a woman chooses to go to prison, she can do that on her own without her man causing her to do so. Enlarging on the subject of domestic violence, in our society today, so many women and men have lost their lives as a result of domestic violence, and even sadder, once death occurs due to domestic violence, the actions that led to death cannot be retracted.

It is easy to get into trouble but can be extremely difficult to get out.

Probably with most people, wisdom accumulates with age due to, if nothing else, an increased number of life experiences of one's own and others'. Now I know that if a man who I have a special relationship with becomes abusive to me, one option at my disposal is calling the police on him and letting the police deal with the abuser. I also do not want to tolerate a man who frequently drinks to intoxication and then becomes crazed. After being through a physically and psychologically abusive relationship, now I would not let myself fall prey to that situation again. I would rather be alone than to endure an abusive relationship with a man. Life has enough "headaches" without the presence of an abusive relationship. I am now tired of being on the lower end of a vicious relationship. As a woman, I think that some men fail to realize that women are just looking for someone to love them, not beat them half to death! My advice is that if one finds herself in a significantly violent relationship, she should get away from it even if she has to leave the city or town. I have had many different types of experiences in my life so far in this world, and have been on both sides of the fence, so to speak. Remember, domestic violence comes in many forms. For examples, there is the psychological abuse like an abusing mate calling the other mate degrading names; and then there is the physical-type abuse such as one mate blackening the other mate's eye(s) or knocking out the other mate's teeth.

I have been told in recent times that I am a sensitive, caring-type person who is highly sociable. I hope that image is accurate. All I want is to have peace of mind and live happily.

It was difficult coming home after being in prison for twenty-two years. I love my family immeasurably and was blessed to be able to spend some time with my parents before they left this world and to be able to interact with my precious children and dear grandchildren. However, I still feel like I am locked up even though I am home now. I still feel lonely within. Time moves on – my children are adults now, living their own lives, and soon my grandchildren will all be grown. Nevertheless, I know that everyone has his or her problems to deal with, so what does a person do? With whom do you talk? Who do you turn to? I have to let go of the things that I cannot change. I guess that is part of life. It would be helpful for a person to acquire good decision-making skills.

Even though I am out of prison now, I often ask myself if I am totally free. Sometimes I still feel like I am a prisoner in a sense because so many people want to be the boss and not a follower and because there seems to be so many rules and regulations in life – a person is allowed to do this but not allowed to do that. There are rules – rules – rules whether a person is in prison or out of prison.

As I have previously written in this book, as an adolescent, I did pretty much what I wanted to. However, now as an adult, I feel that many parents should spend more time with their children to keep their children on the right "path" in life. Presently I see many children watching television far too much of the time which makes them unruly. In a larger sense, I think that the world now is more dangerous than ever before. I think that these days music and a huge number of movies show too much danger to other people along with television shows, for example, *Criminal Minds*.

I could continue endlessly with my present thought about life issues in general, but basically I want people to know what really happened to me that caused me to end up traveling down the wrong "path". Essentially, after my husband was killed I had mental issues and should have sought professional help but did not. Thus, the combination of mental matters and loneliness can produce a severely serious problem(s). This problem is the root that led to a series of events that culminated in me serving a twenty-two-year prison sentence. I wish I could "turn back the hands of time," but I can't. Writing from experience, my advice, especially to adolescents, is to beware of the crowd of people with whom you associate because involvement with these dangerous people makes it much easier to get into trouble.

Moreover, even though I have served my prison time and parole time, when searching for employment, my felony charge in my personal history haunts me; it continues to follow me whenever I encounter a job application. I must say though, a person can successfully surmount that hindrance in his or her past. For example, a person who has a felony in his background became an interim campus president at a community college, so it can be done; it is just exceedingly harder.

Yes, I have another regret. An enormously terrible consequence is that my unwise actions which landed me in prison for twenty-two years not only adversely affected me but also my dearest loved ones – my children and parents. These people were innocent victims of my wrong actions. My wrongdoings and foolish association with an extremely horrible person caused me severe emotional trauma and prolonged agony, but they also produced multiple problems for my children and parents. I was not there in the daily guidance of my children. This arrangement of me being away from my children was most likely the worst during my daughters' adolescent years when they proceeded from childhood to young adulthood which is especially a difficult time for people, possibly especially for females.

Furthermore, for those twenty-two years, I missed family events. By my actions that led to my long imprisonment, I was unable to be an integral part of my children's special events like their high school graduations, their birthday celebrations, the births of their children, share in holiday gatherings, and several other special times. I especially like Christmas; it is such a festive season that promotes a warm togetherness among people.

In spite of my absence, I am exceptionally proud of the way that my three children have turned out. All of them are now fine young ladies. My eldest daughter owns and operates a hair salon and has become a well-known figure in the local hair community. She blends a unique balance of artistry, hairstyles, with a good business sense. My middle daughter, if she would have wanted to, could have most likely become a fashion model but I think sought a more academic interest. She has become a superb paralegal in a local law firm with presently an extensive college background and intends to enroll in law school with the goal of becoming an attorney. My youngest daughter works in law enforcement and is licensed to carry a gun. She has an Associate's degree in criminal justice and is a loving mother and wife. During their formative years, none of them indulged in recreational drugs. There were no significant problems with any of them. Also, all of them have provided me with grandchildren. In addition to my children's own efforts to become responsible and successful citizens, I give much credit to my two wonderful parents who raised my children for those many years that I was incarcerated. When maturing, every child needs guidance, and my dear and capable parents fulfilled that venue. My precious mother seemed to have a real talent for raising children, and my dear father provided a steady atmosphere and labored to provide the necessary money for his loved ones and himself. Furthermore, my sisters and brothers also helped to fill the gaps in my children's lives since I was not actually present in my children's lives for such a long time. As for having a wonderful family, I could ask for nothing more.

I Am Truly Blessed

Beware of the crowd of people with whom you associate because involvement with these dangerous people makes it much easier to get into trouble.

For most people, there is enough natural trouble in their lives, which is just a part of life, without them deliberately causing more trouble for themselves.

It would be helpful for
a person to acquire good
decision-making skills.

I have to let go of
things that I
cannot change.

If a woman chooses to go to prison, she can do that on her own without her man causing her to do so.

Modeling

Marilyn M. Lowery

Personal Relations

I may be contacted for

Fundraisers

Ms. Marilyn Lowery

c/o Seekers Publishing, Inc.

P.O. Box 31630

Independence, Ohio 44131